THE HOUSE REMEMBERS

A childhood on a little farm
at the foot of Galtymore

ANN GARDINER

First published in the Republic of Ireland 2009

Designed, typeset and printed in the European Union
by seamist.graphics@gmail.com

ISBN 978-0-9567084-0-3

Ann and Bobby Gardiner
Tel. 052-67235
Mobile: 087-2855926
gardinerbobby@gmail.com
iamanngardiner@gmail.com

Dedicated to my parents
for the wonderful childhood memories

ACKNOWLEDGEMENTS

This book would never have been finished without the help, support and encouragement of my husband, Bobby, daughters Kelley, Fiodhna, Lynda and sons-in-law Stephen, Padraig and Tom.

I'd also like to thank Rick Myers and Sonia Schorman for their advice and guidance, and to Hugh Stancliffe for his co-ordinating skills in bringing it all together.

A special word of appreciation goes to Dáithí Ó'hÓgáin for taking the time to write the Foreword.

Photographs given for use in the book are acknowledged beside each item. Thank you to Ciarán Breathnach for the cover photo.

The house remembers everything
Of the generations gone
When it's sturdy mortared walls were new
And the golden thatched roof shone
In '32 young John took charge
Along with his new wife
The house closed softly round them
As they started married life

CHORUS

Let's drink a toast to them tonight
And all who've gone before
And the old thatched house that cradled them
Near the slopes of Galtymore

Soon children's voices filled the house
What a glorious din they made
The wood fire blazed when neighbours came
And forty-five was played
The rosary with trimmings too
Rose to the heavens on high
But when he played the old melodeon
The rafters rang with joy

He told us tales of Black and Tans
And the men of '22
O'Malley, Treacy and Dan Breen
His friends so brave and true
They loved their country to the end
And every night would pray
That Ireland would be unified
And prosperous one day

She was broken when she lost him
Lived for many years alone
In that old thatched home they loved so well
Where their children all had grown
But now she's gone to Heaven too
To God's eternal care
The house remembers everything
Standing still and silent there

Repeat CHORUS

CONTENTS

The Gardiner family
(courtesy of Pat McMahon)

INTRODUCTION

The old thatched farmhouse that was our family home for over 150 years recently changed hands. It fell to me to get it ready for the new owners and this included clearing out the dairy, where all kinds of rubbish and discarded household items had been dumped over the years.

The dairy, a big, airy, high-ceilinged shed, was a busy place once. It was here that the separator extracted the cream from the milk, which was then placed in the big wooden churn, with the handle on the side, to make the butter.

But that was all in the past, and here I was now, sitting in the middle of all the clutter wondering what in the name of God I should keep and what was for the skip. As I moved through the cobwebby books, mattresses, broken chairs and antiquated tools memories came flooding back.

Then I had a mad idea. Why not string together all the highlights of growing up on a farm, in the forties and fifties, so that the life of that era could be remembered? The old dairy almost seemed to be whispering encouragement!

With new eyes, I considered the trash and viewed these lost treasures. I wondered why on earth an old light bulb had been preserved. Then I remembered that my parents would never throw anything out. Electricity was a constant source of wonder to them. I thought of when it was first installed and what a difference it made to all our lives.

There were several packs of playing cards still in their boxes on a shelf, which family members had brought back from various trips over the years. My parents must have preferred to use the old ones or else they were saving them for the ultimate card game! What pleasure we extracted from those cards when neighbours came to visit or when we held a special gamble for a goose. And was that the wing with which we used to brush around the fireplace? I thought of when my mother prepared our Christmas goose feast. It also reminded me of my ill-fated Bobby gosling . . .

There were the rosary beads and missal I used in boarding school when we were all fired with devotion and piety. I remembered how cross Mother was if we hadn't our beads ready for the nightly recitation of the rosary. We kept them on a nail on the inside of the closet door near the fire. This must not be confused with the wardrobes in America! Our closet was a built-in hole in the wall which contained all kinds of miscellaneous objects which were ready to fall out when you opened it!

Nervously I peered into dark musty corners with a flash lamp. Electricity had never been installed in here. That would have been considered extravagant! I fell upon a box of *Irelands Own* magazines going back to the 1960s, also some *Our Boys* comics and *Woman's Way* weeklies. I couldn't resist a quick read. As I sat back on a bumpy, damp, mildewed mattress, I was twenty-one again. Did we really wear our skirts that short?

Reading had always been our great escape. We devoured anything we could get our hands on, suitable or not, though my mother kept a close eye. In the absence of radio and television we relied on our imaginations to create drama and excitement.

I was almost afraid to open the old brown trunk, left by some American visitor in the thirties. What if a mouse had taken up residence! Was I ready for the reminders of childhood that might leap out, along with the mouse, to tug at my heart-strings? The thought of Yanks conjured up the excitement of parcels from America. I also remembered the magical year they came to visit when we had to sleep in the dairy. With their painted nails and strange accents we'd never seen creatures so exotic.

All the unwanted items we had conveniently forgotten and left for safe-keeping now came back to haunt me. There was the fancy sugar bowl and jug that Mother won in a raffle and only took out when a T.D. was visiting! Here was a half-hidden, limp shoe-box full of old

Communion, Confirmation and Birthday cards and a diary of my sister Eileen's going back to 1956. Dare I read it?

The box of photographs brought a tear. There was Kathleen, my oldest sister, resplendent in her navy school uniform. Here was one of the whole family posing for a 'Yank' picture. My father had the accordion strapped to his shoulders after playing for a half-set. We loved visitors, though my mother would have been the one with the burden of looking after them. Even in the picture, she had the look of a woman counting chops!

I found dozens of knitting patterns. My mother had marvellous hands and could do many crafts but crotchet was her favourite. She created two beautiful crotchet dresses for me in the sixties and later on items for her grandchildren. As I picked up *Mrs. Beeton's Cookery Book*, the culinary bible of the time, the cellophane paper that my mother kept for covering burns fell out.

I tripped over a half-concealed, two-pronged pike with a broken handle, used for haymaking in the sunny long ago. In my father's time things were always repaired, not thrown out. He set aside wet days for fixing broken farm implements and also putting soles on our shoes.

Eileen's brown covered copybooks revealed her copperplate Irish writing. What pride we had in our work. It was the old form with the *seimhiu*, which has been replaced by the 'h' for some fifty years. My Legion of Mary manual stirred memories of life in Dublin, when I was still in my religious phase. Should I keep it? There was the black bound thesis that Kathleen had sent to my mother after she did her degree. Did she ever read it? Who knows? But the poor woman couldn't possibly throw it away.

I decided the old horses' collar and winkers hanging on a crook were worth rescuing though. What doors were opened in my mind of Dolly, the gentle white mare, being tackled, when she took us to Mass and to town.

How often had my mother painstakingly washed the eggs and laid them in hay in the handmade brown wicker basket, which now almost fell apart in my hands when I touched it.

I found old plant holders, cracked cups and holy pictures of Mary and various saints, letters, newspapers and postcards. There were some balls of twine vying for space with rolls of wire, a box of dusty jam jars and a pair of wellingtons. This was the footwear commonly worn around the farm by both men and women. From all the items, it was my mother's little short rubber wellingtons that brought up the past most poignantly.

I suddenly wondered what had become of the green wooden aeroplane that my father had made in the forties. A more recent addition was the small yellow tent I'd taken up to Galtymore, along with a very reluctant husband. I'd hardly need that again!

As I straightened my tired, aching back and brushed off the dust and cobwebs, I took a look around. The dairy would take another day's work. In the meantime, I had a lot to consider.

FOREWORD

Dáithí Ó hÓgáin is a native of Bruff, Co Limerick. He is the author of many books, including poetry, short stories and research works. He is Professor of Irish Folklore at University College, Dublin,

There are many different kinds of writers, but I suppose that basically one can divide them all into two basic types. The first type challenges readers with the style, using metaphors and other indirect devices to bring them to the atmosphere and perspective that is intended. The second type is direct, using clear sentences which give information on the subject, illustrating reality and evoking the appropriate feelings. Ann Gardiner belongs to the second category. That is not to say, of course, that the qualities of a writer ultimately depend for good or for ill on the technique employed. Almost any technique can give good writing and impart interesting material, depending on the natural ability, the artistic commitment, and the inherent honesty and good nature of the author. The practice of writing is, despite is frequent misrepresentation both by practitioners and critics, a straightforward enough undertaking, and a worthy one, which will remain so as long as people believe in sharing insights and in genially pursuing the aim of knowing life better.

I say all of this by way of introducing Ann Gardiner, whose personality, honesty and gentle humour spring from every page of this book. Born Ann Kearney in Burncourt, every part of her life has been captured by her vivid memory, and the qualities of her people – generous, sensible, wise, learned, self-effacing – have all come to fruition in this work. Her style is homely and lively, her great gift is minuteness of description and a keen sense of the moment. Her writing has something of a camera-quality, and that is very valuable for all of us who wish to learn. With her, we observe and experience the actions, which show character, we hear the voices, we sense the occasion, and we see the shades of light and the mingling of colours.

I believe that the often-used word 'culture' is best interpreted as how we humanise our surroundings. Given our nature and potential, the process is perennial to us as people, and it can always be bright and fulfilling if only we will have it so. Let's be straight and direct about it – there is far too much writing around which portrays people as nasty and depraved beings, far too much ignoring in ink and print of finer vistas in which the human spirit shows how misfortune can be endured and overcome. We should remember the potential that is always present, wherever we are. Every part of everywhere has fine imagery and promise when the environment and the human spirit are in tandem. Every part of Ireland, for example, has its own special appeal and its own thrill in being involved in it. It is very beautiful in south Tipperary when the sun is shining, not only in the sky but in our hearts as well – the luscious fields, the homely villages, the majestic mountain slopes, the proud history and the generous disposition of the inhabitants.

Something of all of this can be gleaned from the book, in which the author speaks to us with a special and individualistic mind. Readers who come from her area, those at home and those in faraway countries and continents, will get a feeling for their youth and for the place which formed much of their personality and character. They can have the pleasure of being there again, even if only in the imagination, and it should not be forgotten that the imagination is a great force for our well-being and happiness. This immediacy gives the book its special affectionate character, but there is more, for as a social document of the past generation it contains many samples of sentiment, many truths forgotten or partly so or now misunderstood, many illustrations of life and problems and happenings and fun. The experience of spending our youth in a rural community is one shared by very many of us, the type of education we got from our parents, neighbours and teachers which is too often under-rated nowadays, the going away in a poignant mixture of sadness and expectation, and sometimes the return which allows all opinions to be tested.

Ann describes with verve and no small amount of humour the life lived by many of us for several years in urban flatlands, the sense of independence that we enjoyed but which alternated with a searing

longing for the community life with different accents and different
sensitivities – all of course inherent in the rich variety if place and
custom which is the human experience. And then there is the lyrical
note – her romance with the brilliant traditional musician Bobby
Gardiner who became her husband, the gentle teasing of his dislike
of climbing mountains which is considered in her native area as a test
of youthful vigour (Bobby is a native of the faraway and alien County
Clare!), not to mention the joy of rearing children in a happy family.

On the broader plane, it can be said that Ann Gardiner represents
our success in maintaining continuity between past and present in
Ireland. Her own young family reflects the same basic values as the
family who reared her, new sentiment reflects the old in changing
circumstances, the spirit of human feeling persists and stretches into
the future. This is a book which upholds all of that, which is quiet in
its confidence, fulfilling rather than deceptive in its simplicity, and
most of all enjoyable in its reading. A great native of her area over
three hundred years ago out it succinctly. He was Seathrun Ceitinn,
priest and theologian, scholar and poet, and a hero in Tipperary folk
tradition. His lines of well-wishing were composed when leaving
Ireland in his youth, but he was fortunate enough to return, and his
words are of value in either context:

> *Mo shlán dá mághaibh míne, slán fé mhíle da cnoca,*
> *Mochean don té ata ínti, slán dá línnte is dá locha!*
> *Slán dá coillte fé thorthaí, slán fós dá corthaí iascaigh*
> *Slán dá mointe is dáb anta, slán dá rathaí is dá riascai!*

> *(My good wish to her gentle plains, a thousand wishes to her hills;*
> *Fortunate for him who is there, may her pools and her lakes fare well!*
> *May her woods under fruit fare well, also may her fishing weirs;*
> *May her moors and her fields fare well, her moats and her marshes!)*

These are the kinds of images, moving through the landscape and
hovering over the experiences. This is the voice of the author, the
atmosphere that one finds in this book. The pictures are coming into
view, the people are talking . . .

Dáithí Ó hÓgáin

A WORD ABOUT MY PARENTS

My mother, Hannah Casey, was born in 1903 in Carrigeen, near Kilbehenny, Co. Limerick, about five miles from where she would eventually settle down. She was the second youngest of twelve children, four boys and eight girls, many of whom emigrated to either England or America.

She walked four miles to Skeheenarinky (which translates as 'the little dancing bush') school every day, where her brother Tom was one of the teachers, past the famous Galty castle, home to the Buckley family. She had a secret wish to be a teacher too, but never voiced it, knowing that her widowed mother had many demands on her limited resources. On the way home, Hannah often watched the ladies playing tennis on the lawn of the castle or she might slip into the kitchen, where her older sister was a cook, in the hope of getting a little treat. She was a bright student and loved her school days. After finishing, she spent some time in Glin, Co. Limerick with her brother Tim and his wife, both of whom taught in Ballyguiltanane, where she cared for their three young boys.

Hannah could be described as 'a fine figure of a woman'. Pale, skinny girls were not much in demand. There was always a suspicion that they might be harbouring the dreaded consumption. Nor were the men of that era taken in by lots of powder and paint! They liked their women with rosy cheeks and a healthy, natural, appearance.

My father, John Kearney, was born in 1895 in the old thatched farmhouse, near Burncourt, Co. Tipperary, the youngest of four children, two boys and two girls. The others emigrated to the U.S.A. Aunt Ciss settled in Dorchester, Aunt Bab entered a convent in Rutland, Vermont and his brother Tom was an architect in Boston. John was destined to become a farmer. Whether he liked it or not! He went to school in

Burncourt (*An Cuirt Doite*) named after the castle built by the Everard family in 1641 which subsequently got burnt.

Something momentous happened in the village in June 1903, when John was just a small boy. King Edward VII of England was passing through on his way to Shanballa Castle, a few miles away. People came out in large numbers to get a glimpse of the king and his entourage. Somebody set a gramophone playing near the road to add to the festivities and there was a great sense of anticipation and excitement in the air. The children, including John, were lined up on the road outside the school to salute his royal highness as he went by. John recalls however that he was far more interested in the gramophone, a thing he'd never seen before, than in the royal visitor! In light of his views on the British occupation and his republican leanings later on, I think he might have regretted saluting the king at all!

It's worth remembering that Shanballa Castle was once a familiar landmark in the lush farmlands between Burncourt and Clogheen. Its imposing towers and turrets rose skywards for over 130 years against the backdrop of the majestic Knockmealdown mountains. The castle was designed by the famous architect, John Nash, and built in 1812 for Cornelius O'Callaghan, Baron of Lismore and later passed on to his cousin Lady Beatrice Pole-Carew. By all accounts it was a magnificent building, inside and out, and one of Ireland's finest castles. It boasted a huge staff and gave much needed employment to the local people. Sadly it was demolished in March 1960 and the land divided. They say that politics and greed may have contributed to its demise. My father always maintained that enough wasn't done to save this lovely cut stone building which would be a national treasure if we had it today.

Growing up, John was almost like an only child, and a great pet with his mother. She would take him to Mitchelstown in the pony and trap for fiddle lessons, to the well-known maestro, Jimmy Fitzgerald. John also played melodeon and accordion and was much sought after at threshing and gamble dances.

Sadly, he would never again see his sister, who entered the convent in Rutland, Vermont, or his brother Tom again. Aunt Ciss visited a

Dan Breen

couple of times over the years. These were the heart breaking days of the American wakes, when families were separated very young, sometimes forever, with the familiar red and blue airmail letters their only connection.

John became embroiled in the War of Independence in the early 1920s and received his IRA training from such legendary figures as Dan Breen, Sean Treacy, Ernie O'Malley and Seamus Robinson. He commanded the Skeheenarinky Company up to the time of the truce and later during the Civil War. His company was mostly involved in destroying bridges and tearing up roads, thus making travel difficult for British armoured cars. One fateful night my father almost lost his life. A bridge he was knocking collapsed under him and he fell into the river, but fortunately, a friend jumped in and saved him.

Like many others of the company, John took the anti-treaty side in the Civil War and suffered much privation because of this. He was arrested in November 1922 and spent five months in Clonmel jail, three months in Kilkenny prison, where he underwent a twelve day hunger strike, and a month in Harepark camp, Kildare. My grandparents and my granduncle, Fr. O'Connor, went to the prison begging my father to surrender, but he refused. It wasn't until 1923, when the Civil War ended, that he returned to working the farm again.

He maintained a life long friendship with Dan Breen with whom he corresponded regularly over the years. Thankfully, we preserved several of Dan's letters. My sister Kathleen remembers getting a half-crown from him one time at Mulvey's pub in Araglin and John got a shilling, which my parents made into a medal. However the half-crown was too valuable to keep!

THIS HISTORIC PICTURE, taken in 1920, and kindly lent by Mr. Michael Hanrahan, Castlegrace, Clogheen, shows officers of the 6th Battalion, 3rd Tipperary Brigade, Second Southern Division, I.R.A.
BACK ROW (left to right)—Wm. O'Connor, Rehill (now in U.S.A.); Capt., K.Coy.; G. O'Dwyer, Ballycloghet; Capt., A.Coy.; C. Conway, Burncourt, Director of Training; John Kearney, Skeheenarinky, Capt., D.Coy.; Maurice O'Gorman, Ballybacon, Capt., B.Coy.
CENTRE—Thomas O'Connor, Garrymore, Capt., E.Coy.; Michael McGrath, Skeheenarinky, First Lieut., D.Coy.; Jack Ryan (deceased), Burncourt, Capt., G.Coy.; Sean Myles, Graigue and Ballylooby, Vice-Comdt. 6th Battalion; Pat O'Donnell, Castlegrace (now in U.S.), Capt., C.Coy.; John Donoghue (deceased), Cahir, First Lieut., H.Coy.; Michael O'Mahony, Ballylooby, Lieut. of Transport, 6th Batt.; Wm. O'Connor (deceased), Garrymore, Second Lieut., H.Coy.
IN FRONT—Ed. McNamara (deceased), Ardfinnan, Engineer, 6th Batt.; Tom Lynch (deceased), Tipperary, Asst. Brig. Adj.; Sean Prendergast (deceased), Ballybacon), Comdr., 6th Batt.; Thos. O'Gorman, Ballyporeen, Capt., F.Coy.; Thos. O'Mahony, Ballylooby, Intelligence Officer, 6th Batt.

The Fighting Sixth – John Kearney is in the back row, fourth from left.

John Kearney met Hannah Casey some time in the mid to late twenties. In order to be on time for dates up by the Galty castle, he would put the old clock in the kitchen forward, as otherwise his father would keep him working outside till all hours! On the 3rd of August 1932 they got married in Westland Row church, Dublin with their bridesmaid and best man in attendance. After a week's honeymoon, they returned to begin their married life on the newly-handed-over farm, with my father's parents still in residence.

They got along well and had a good life, rearing and educating four children – John, Kathleen, Eileen and Ann, from the meagre returns of a small farm. They enjoyed the simple life; meeting friends and neighbours; going for outings to visit relatives and playing cards.

With the absence of running water and electricity, and any kind of mechanisation on the farm, all the work was done by hand, and my father had to be a jack-of-all-trades. Like everybody of that time, they couldn't have saved the hay or threshed the corn without the help of the neighbours.

My father broke his leg in a farmyard accident in the mid-forties and it was while he was recovering in Clogheen hospital that his name was put forward to run in the local election. He wasn't able to travel around the constituency to canvass votes but he made it anyway. He was a most conscientious councillor. I remember how, every Sunday for years, he'd pull a small table up to the fire and spend the day writing to Dail Eireann and County engineers trying to get roads fixed, bridges built and cottages allocated to needy people

'Is it one c and two s's in necessary?' he might ask, peering over his glasses. My mother always had the answer. Her spelling was impeccable. The expenses for being a councillor were very meagre at the time and there was no account taken of stationery or stamps, but nonetheless, it never stopped my father from having his little bundle of envelopes ready for the post on Monday morning! Because of his involvement in the County Council he made frequent trips to Clonmel, Thurles and even to Dublin to attend the Fianna Fáil *Árd Fheiseanna*. He once went to Sligo which seemed an awful distance away to me!

My mother loved to read when the household chores were finished at night. She enjoyed Annie Smithson's books because they were 'clean' and had a good moral. She was very strict about what we read. I remember that she disapproved of the classic *Jane Eyre* because the heroine was in love with a married man! My father was on the library committee in Thurles and Mother set herself up as a censor, reporting any writing of a questionable nature or with coarse language.

Dad liked the *Ireland's Own* and would read it from cover to cover, laughing over the jokes and riddles. As we got older, sometimes, he'd call out a request for a pen pal at the back of the magazine and slyly wait for our reaction! Irish television was there for a short time before

John and Hannah in the 1950s

he died and he enjoyed Maureen Potter, Jimmy O'Dea and news programmes. However, it never replaced the satisfaction he got from playing cards or music!

My parents drew great strength and consolation from their faith and never failed to go to Mass and the sacraments. The rosary was a nightly ritual from which no one, including neighbours who chanced

*Top to bottom: Burncourt Castle, Shanballa Castle (both courtesy of John
Tuohy), Galty Castle (courtesy of Carol De Falco and Ed Riordan)*

to visit, was excused. But prayers were not confined to Sundays. They spilled over into ordinary life. As my father drove to town in the pony and trap, and later in the car, he would tip his cap and make the sign of the cross as he passed particular gateways and old houses.

'God bless Mike' he'd say, or 'The Lord have mercy on Will', or' God be good to Jim'. He might then launch into reminiscences about neighbours who had passed away.

His great joy was his first car, bought in 1952. Although he was a less than perfect driver, having only the sight of one eye, his confidence, (and my mother's prayers!) brought him safely through! He died before his time, in 1964 from pancreatic cancer after an illness of six months. He was waked in the parlour of the old thatched house.

My mother had a long life and lived alone in her beloved home, with its quiet, peaceful surroundings, apart from short visits to family members. She died in hospital in 1995, following a stroke.

My parents were proud of their Irishness. They loved the customs, traditions, superstitions and music of the country. They had a great interest in the Irish language, even though they couldn't speak it. However, their conversations were peppered with Irish words and expressions, a legacy of a previous generation who spoke the language fluently. I hope we inherited some of their values. Like respect for people, nature, animals and the countryside

And the capacity to enjoy the simple things of life!

AS IT WAS IN THE BEGINNING

Running scared from the hissing gander as he stretched out his long white neck . . . Listening, cosy and safe to the rain drumming down on the galvanised roof of the car-house; the bedraggled hens running in for shelter as they tried to fluff up their feathers.

We were all born in the parlour of our old thatched farmhouse in the fertile valley between the Galty and Knockmealdown mountains in Co. Tipperary. The house had shelter on all sides, my father being a great man for setting groves of trees.

There was a nice glass porch in front, outside which our childhood photographs were taken. There's one old black and white picture of me, on my first Communion Day, squinting up at the sun in my white dress and veil. Since we were situated two fields in from the road, over a little bridge that crossed the Sheep river you could say that we were rather isolated. Americans would call it charming and secluded. To us it was just home and it was years before we would learn to appreciate its scenic appeal.

I imagine my mother picked the parlour for her confinements because it was a large airy room and presentable enough for the district nurse. With the reserve and stoicism of her generation, the birthing process was never discussed. At least not with us!! At any rate, the district nurse duly arrived with her black bag and all the small knitted baby clothes were put airing to the fire on the back of the sugán chair. My brother, John and two older sisters, Kathleen and Eileen, were convinced that she brought the baby in the bag. After being closeted in the parlour with my mother and the boiled water for a period of time, the nurse emerged triumphantly with the roaring new addition.

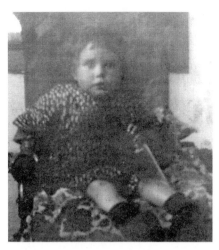

Ann as a baby

I was born on the eve of my sister Eileen's fourth birthday and when my mother gave her a choice between the new baby and an orange, she immediately decided in favour of the fruit! By all accounts, I was stubborn and self-willed. I would knock on the porch door to get in, when I was too small to open the door myself, and if anybody, other than my mother, came I would bang the door shut again shouting 'Mam ope!'

One time, Mother spent hours making a beautiful dress for my doll, complete with the latest fashionable puffed sleeves. I got a notion that I didn't like the sleeves and when her back was turned I threw the lovely dress into the fire. Imagine her disappointment after the hours she'd worked on it! She later made us a big doll out of an old shirt of my father's. We christened her Mary Alice! Stuffed with straw, she had a wild stare in her knitted eyes and a crooked grinning mouth, but we loved her anyway and had her as a baby in our cabby-houses for a while. She came to a bad end when we forgot to take her in out of the wet!

Another day in Mitchelstown, my mother asked me to hold her handbag for a second and I'm told that I boldly threw it down the street after her. I must have been a little horror!

Even though we were not near the road or other houses, our yard, orchard, garden and fields were lively places and I never felt lonely. Ducks, geese, hens, dogs, cats and magpies vied for space and food in the yard in front of the house. I often spent hours out there eating my bread and jam and watching their antics. The chopping block was there also, where my father cut the bushes and sticks for the fire. Occasionally, my mother would use it to chop the head off a young cock for the Sunday dinner. The pig's day of reckoning would come too!

The first shoes and socks that were bought for me must have coincided with my early attempts at talking because I would perform my party piece for visitors, which went: 'I got shoes for two and a levvy and socks for dillon!' (This translates as shoes for 2/11 and socks for a shilling.)

Being the youngest, I probably got away with stuff the others didn't. But I had to make up for that by trying to be funny – singing, dancing and being generally outrageous. This irresponsible image backfired of course. It would be years before anybody took me seriously or listened to anything I had to say!

John, my older brother, who was just developing an interest in writing, recorded the baby's amusing sayings. You could say I was his first inspiration! It was called 'The funny sayings and doings of little Ann'! When my parents would return from town all the messages were laid out on the big kitchen table. I was too small to see over the top, so I would crane my neck to look for brown paper bags that might have sweets.

When our father was in Clogheen hospital after breaking his leg, I was brought to visit him and asked to dance for the nuns. After a few evenings of this I got fed up, and said I had a sore leg. The nun said to me, 'Show us how you could dance before you hurt your leg, Ann'. And of course I got caught out! Mother would lift me up at night, in front of the Sacred Heart picture, and we'd pray for Dad in hospital. The prayer went: 'Baby Jesus make Daddy's leg all right so he can do his work for little Ann.'

My grandfather was living in the house with us when I was little and when rosary time came I would pay a visit to his room to escape the boring prayers in the kitchen. These were all pre-school days, so my memories of him aren't as clear as those of my older sisters and brother, to whom he spoke Irish. When he died, he was waked in the parlour, so once again this room served its noble purpose. I remember how the big field around our house was thronged with ponies, traps, bicycles and people. It was very exciting and I wasn't sad at all.

I climbed the ladder to my bed in the loft each night and there was no fear of me causing any trouble or falling out, as I had a sister at each side to literally keep me in my place. We were lulled to sleep by the rustling of mice or wind in the thatch, and the comforting murmur of our parents' voices as they sat by the fire going over the day's events. One night I threatened to tell on my sister who woke up thirsty and drank the holy water from the font in the room. It would have been a great tale for mother's ears but I couldn't chance taking the risk!

Small children weren't taken out very much that time. It wasn't until I was going to school that I saw the big world beyond our road gate. My sister, Kathleen, wondered why my mother didn't take the pram to town when I was small, so that I could be paraded up and down the street like a town baby. I think Mother had probably quite enough to do, driving the pony and trap the long eight miles to Mitchelstown, without taking our pram. It had probably seen better days anyway, after three other children!

The house, yard, orchard and fields were my world at that time and I knew every nook, cranny and hiding hole intimately. I was on first name terms with the cows, horses and donkey. I had a cabby, or play-house with the dog, cat and dolls as my children. The most important piece of equipment was a big stick to keep them all in order. They got their dinner served on bits of 'chainies' (pieces of old broken crockery). The dolls were no bother but the cat and dog had a tendency to wander off!

We practised our plays in the pig shed. John drew pictures of Wolfe Tone and Robert Emmett on the whitewashed cow house. We enjoyed listening to my mother singing as she coaxed a white stream of milk from Judy, the placid red cow. Mooey, the black Friesian was another matter, and had to be spancelled as she often sent the bucket and its contents flying.

I visited the henhouse regularly to collect the eggs and inspect the hatching hen, sitting importantly in a hay-lined black pot, hatching eggs. Mam said that they were excellent mothers. A hen would have to be lifted every day from the nest to do her business and be fed.

She would rather die than leave those eggs unattended. Any time I went near her she would fix me with her beady eye, making warning, clucking noises. How I willed her to hurry up! There was nothing as exciting as a fluffy chicken. Except perhaps, a baby gosling . . .

Neighbours would ask me, 'What will you do when you're big?'

I hadn't given this much thought. Then one day, I decided I wanted to be a shop-keeper And I knew what I wanted to do with my money. I wanted to buy a pair of glasses, a good sleeping doll and a corset!

I didn't know very many small children, except for occasional visits from cousins. And then we were too shy to interact! I would peep shyly from behind my mother's skirt, longing to ask them to come out to play with the new pups but always leaving it too late. A baby was an even greater novelty to me. Being the youngest, I lost count of the prayers I offered up each night that God would send us a new baby. But he never did! Not being familiar with the facts of life, I didn't realise that the fact that my mother was well over forty by then narrowed the chances quite considerably!

Now that I had familiarised myself with my immediate environment, I was ready to take on the next, very important stage of life. I was ready for school!

CAREFREE SCHOOL DAYS

The journey back and forth to school was an adventure in itself; watching rabbits darting out of holes, looking for birds' nests and wild berries, visiting the old reclusive lady on the boreen, singing and making up stories ...

I was nearly seven years old when I started school. Being the youngest and the pet, my parents were loath to part with me. At least, that's what I liked to think! The truth was that a certain measure of strength and stamina were required before I could negotiate the two-mile walk each way.

My mother made me a cloth school bag for my bottle of milk and bread and butter sandwich. so I was all set and ready for the big adventure. It would probably be my first time leaving the old thatched house without my mother. The leave-taking protocol in our house was the same as long as I remember. You splashed some holy water on your forehead from the font on your way out, made the sign of the cross and shouted 'Good luck'. At first, my older sisters and brother were excited at the novelty of bringing me to school. I was shown the various short cuts. They pushed me through fields, dragged me over ditches and across rivers and squeezed me through thorny hedges. Their interest in me didn't last however, when they found that I was slowing them down and making them late!

The school itself was a fine old limestone building erected by the Buckley family, who had been the area's resident landlords and had lived in the Galty Castle many years before. It was the same school that my mother had attended. The three teachers, though unrelated, were all called Casey. I was put in the same classroom as my sister for the first few days, so I wouldn't be lonely. Miss Casey gave me a shiny new penny. She was a well-upholstered, gentle, easy-going lady. She gathered us around her like a clutch of chickens, teaching us our prayers and tables and preparing us for the exciting road to knowledge.

We progressed from playing with *márla*, or plasticine, to laboriously chalking our letters and numbers on the black slates that Miss Casey divided out amongst us. We did small addition and subtraction sums as well and rubbed them out with our fists or the sleeves of our jumpers, as necessary! I was thrilled when at last the words in the storybooks came alive. Up to then, I had to content myself with composing my own stories from the pictures.

Approaching our first confession, Miss Casey had us well-tutored. We had a practice run and we gathered up

Ann's First Communion

a fine collection of sins. We learned our act of contrition. Some of the bold boys had their own version that went as follows:

An act of contrition, my father went fishin'!

Oh my God, he broke the rod!'

The most remarkable thing about my first Communion day, for me, was that my mother decided I should wear two sets of underwear under my white dress. She was afraid that I'd get pneumonia travelling to the church in the pony and trap! I was longing for a pair of white shoes to go with the dress but they were considered impractical for wearing afterwards so I wore black patent ones instead. Nobody gave me any money or made a fuss. The dress and veil were enough excitement.

Flush toilets came to our school in the early fifties. Miss Casey brought us out, in groups, to inspect this great wonder, instructing us on the quantity of toilet roll sheets we should use!

The 'Top Road' was the preferred route home from school as it had more traffic, shops and houses. It also meant I had my friend Mary for company part of the way. Sometimes we stopped at her gate and played with her doll, Matilda, which she got with her father's cigarette coupons. Matilda had a green velvet dress and could open and close her eyes. I hoped and prayed that some time Santa Claus would bring me one like it. The last bit of my journey was down a boreen past the house of an odd, contrary old lady. I'd sometimes meet her, dressed in her long black clothes, gathering bits of sticks for the fire or I might drop in to her house for a chat. My mother discouraged my visits. Consumption had taken its toll in that house, like many others of the time.

Our parents urged us to take the safer 'Low Road' but we found it rather quiet and dreary. Except when the wild strawberries were plentiful in the hedges! We also knew where to look for cherries, whorts (wild blueberries) and hazel nuts. We seemed to take forever to get home and our mother was often worried accusing us of 'cadaying' around the road! On hot summer days, we dispensed with shoes and dug our toes into the soft black tarry road. Butter was rubbed into our feet to soften the tar. This, combined with a vigorous scrubbing, was necessary before we were fit to go to bed!

Around this time, the school lost a member of staff and I was catapulted into the master's room a bit prematurely. He must have had four classes in his room, which couldn't have been easy. I was always late for school. I blamed it on the clock, which had a habit of being slow. The rolls would invariably be called as I tried to sneak unnoticed into my place, but the Master always caught me. He would fix me with a malevolent stare, remarking, sarcastically *'do thangais'* meaning 'you came'. He never punished me. He taught all subjects through Irish. If you needed a copybook and didn't know the Irish word you had to ask *'Cad é an gaeilge atá ar* copybook'? He was a native of west Cork – a wonderful teacher who did his best to pass on his love of the language to his pupils. His teaching of Irish history was inspiring and unashamedly biased!

Lunchtime was for socialising and consolidating friendships. After we'd eaten our bread and butter and drunk our milk from the cough bottle we'd carefully washed, we packed as much fun and games as possible into the remainder of the half hour break. We loved to play cabby-house. We picked the most appealing and co-operative of the junior infants for our babies. I found it great to have such a pool to pick from after having only the cat and dog at home! We were busy little mothers, marking off the rooms with rows of stones, sweeping the clay floor clean with a furze brush and arranging our cups with great care.

One time there was a catastrophe! The boys burst through our cabby-house, throwing everything into disarray and scattering our 'chainies' in all directions. We were inconsolable. Surprisingly, the Master took our complaint seriously and held a court. In the course of questioning I was asked

'Where were you when the boys attacked?'

'In the kitchen, sir', I answered tearfully.

The teacher, keeping a straight face, came to his judicial conclusions and ordered the boys to apologise. Justice was served!

At other times, we played at saying Mass but everyone wanted to be the priest! Hide-and-go-seek, Red Rover and various ball games activated our competitive spirit as well as keeping us warm in the winter. The older, sixth class girls, walked around with arms linked, sharing secrets. They thought they were getting too big now for the rough and tumble of the playground. When the Master clapped his hands we all trooped back to the classroom.

I got the whooping cough when I was in fifth class and spent a month at home. Mother tended to me day and night and was very worried. It was the only time I had a visit from the doctor and I feared it was a bad sign! To pass the time, I decided to invent my own language. How difficult could it be? '**Rica fore fe cacio**' meant turn on the wireless and '*rica fer fe cacio*' meant to turn it off. I felt very clever and wrote out all my nonsensical made up words and sentences. I roped in the whole family and insisted that they learn off

School pals in the 1940s – Ann is second from left

the phrases. But they only laughed at me, so my hopes of becoming famous evaporated into thin air!

Religious Examination day was very important in our school. The priest's purpose in visiting was to assess the religious knowledge of the children. We would have been preparing for weeks before. Woe betide the child who hadn't a new dress to wear for that important occasion. I wasn't at all concerned about the religion questions!

Christian brothers and nuns called to the school from time to time, creating a welcome distraction. We were told about the missions and the plight of the black babies and the need for religious vocations. On one occasion, my twelve-year-old brother, among others, put up his hand volunteering to become a Christian brother in Africa. My parents had a dilemma on their hands. Much as they disliked the idea of their only son, maybe out there in the jungle, far from home, who were they to fly in the face of God and deny him his vocation. They conferred with the parish priest. He very wisely told them to go home and have sense and forget about the missions. Wasn't he wanted on the farm? My brother's transient vocation was never heard of again. But he didn't become a farmer either!

The highlight of our year was the threshing of the corn and we would ask the Master for permission to go home early on that day. We practised asking *as gaeilge* to get in his good books. He never refused and what an amazing evening of lemonade and dancing and a kitchen full of neighbours was in store.

Our summer holidays were well filled with chores on the farm, saving the hay and thinning turnips. Our greatest luxury was to sneak away to read a book, because if mother spotted you idle – and reading a book was considered idle – you'd be sure to get a job. There was water to be drawn from the river, chickens to feed, wood to gather or a fire to tend. Sometimes, we would hide in the lavatory in the orchard to read!

The primary certificate examination signalled the end of school. We had to travel to Ballyporeen to the convent for this test, which was a one-day exam for the three papers. There were three subjects examined, Irish, English and Maths. The main things they tested in English were essay-writing, letter-writing and comprehension by answering a set of questions and a section known as parsing and analysis, where the pupil was expected to identify the parts of speech in a sentence. This was the same for the Irish paper. There were two Maths papers. The main areas were problem solving, fractions, simple interest and a bill. The second Maths paper was mental arithmetic. I was never more frightened of any exam before or since. I was sure I'd fail my sums! It seems there was no detailed breakdown of results given – it was either pass or fail. This was the only piece of paper most children had to show to prove their numeracy and literacy skills to a prospective employer. It was a very important document. If you were lucky enough to be going on to secondary school, it also provided an entry qualification.

At this stage, many people finished with school, back in the fifties, and emigrated to England, the United States and Australia. The primary cert was abolished around 1967, as by then, most young people were availing of second-level education with the advent of school buses.

I have nothing but good memories of my time in that primary school which set me on the road to knowledge! I never got a slap and have nothing but praise for those dedicated teachers who started me off on the road to learning. May they enjoy a place in Heaven. There are many of my classmates whom I've never laid eyes on since then and a few have passed away. However, their names and faces are indelibly etched on my mind. Eternally young.

LIVING WITH A GOSLING

A gosling is so soft and fragile that it would tug at any child's heart. You want to love and protect it. My gosling thought I was its mother and followed me everywhere, much to the disgust of the gander! This gosling (that I named Bobby gosling) lived in the house with us and because we had cement floors and whitewashed walls nobody was bothered if he made a mess. It could never happen today!

'I think this little fellow might need a bit of extra care,' smiled my mother, handing me a soft scrap of down, feathers and yellow beak.

I was delighted. Having taken care of a few delicate goslings before, I knew the joy this one would bring. I have to admit that my track record of restoring their health wasn't great. But this time it would be different. I lifted up the small soft ball of green fluff and promised I'd be his best friend. My ten-year-old heart was bursting with excitement and happiness as I imagined the fun we'd have together. The summer holidays had just begun, and I had been promoted to the lofty realms of third class.

I felt free as a bird as I raced about in my white canvas shoes and white-spotted dress. Dad would have a few jobs lined up on the farm, but other than that I would have the whole summer to enjoy my new gosling. I chose a cosy spot by the fire for the gosling's cardboard box, which I filled with straw.

'Do you think that he will stay in that?' laughed my mother, but in no time at all, he waddled in and out of the box, all by himself.

Father was the one in our house who lit the fire, so he was usually the first one up. Bobby gosling would sit companionably beside him, chirping away to Dad, who would stroke the gosling's soft downy head, the little eyes drooping with pleasure. Our parents had great time for our pets and entered whole-heartedly into welcoming the new family member.

The gosling got fatter and healthier by the day from the scraps of meal, eggs and bread I hand-fed him. I sometimes had to scold him for pecking the whitewash off the kitchen wall. Secretly, however, I thought he was the smartest, most amazing creature ever and delighted in every move he made!

One day, the gosling tucked inside my jumper, we visited Molly who lived across the river with brothers Tom and Jack. They were elderly and had never married and had an insatiable appetite for gossip. Molly kept a terribly untidy house. The kitchen floor was littered with boxes, buckets, brushes and bags and the table was covered with unwashed dishes. While I answered her never-ending barrage of questions regarding the productivity of my mother's hens, how many cows were calved, if we'd heard from the Yanks, the gosling was exploring Molly's kitchen with great interest.

'What have we here?' exclaimed Molly in astonishment as she watched my pet picking his way around her boxes and brushes. 'Where does he sleep? Does your mother give him the run of the house? What does he eat? I was delighted to talk on my favourite topic. But suddenly there was no sign of the gosling and I couldn't start rooting through the kitchen in search of him. Then, a sleepy-looking yellow head popped up out of a bag of meal. He needed no supper that night!

My aunt Julia, however, was less than thrilled when I brought the gosling to visit. She kept an extremely tidy house and presided over very important business that occurred at the same time each day, which claimed her undivided attention. This event was 'Jack's Dinner'. The diminutive, feisty little woman fussed and bustled round the kitchen like one possessed, peeling vegetables, looking into pots, laying out plates, brushing everything in her way aside. Jack, though twice her height was mightily in awe of her.

'You came at a bad time', declared my aunt crossly. 'And why didn't you leave the duck at home after you? He'd better not leave his card on my clean floor.' The gosling peered into Aunt Julia's nooks and crannies with great interest, oblivious of the fuss. I was getting uneasy. 'Still', continued my aunt slyly, 'I suppose if you feed him up good, he'll make a decent Christmas dinner.' I quickly scooped my gosling into my arms, stuck my tongue out at my aunt, made for the door, vowing never to visit her again!

When we walked down the fields to meet Maurice, the postman, the gosling ignored his goose family completely. The gander was not impressed, hissing threateningly at me. I had a previous run-in with the same gander and was relieved to see the postman approaching. He laughed, when he saw the gosling with outstretched wings, running to keep up with me

My pet was becoming something of a celebrity. When the card-players came on Sunday nights, my gosling would have to be paraded for their amusement. I basked, with a proprietorial air, in their admiration. I didn't want this gosling to grow into a goose, or the summer to ever end . . .

Bobby gosling created a welcome distraction at the nightly rosary as we watched his antics. My mother would be too immersed in her prayers to notice the laughing and carry on as we played with the little fellow. It was on one such night that disaster struck. A couple of us, giddy children, overturned the long wooden bench. It fell on Bobby gosling, crushing the life out of him. Tearfully, I took him up, hoping to preserve the poor broken body. It was no use.

The rosary continued, uninterrupted, while my world ended. Next morning as I cried bitter tears I wrapped my gosling in an old jumper and buried him under an apple tree in the orchard. I still feel lonely, all those years later, when I think about him.

DON'T BRING IN THE CHICKENS

It's a big lesson for a child to learn that actions have consequences and that rules are there for a reason! We hadn't yet learned to be responsible for something more helpless than ourselves . . .

'Be careful with the fire now, don't go near the gramophone and whatever you do, don't bring in the new baby chickens.' My mother issued her usual last minute instructions as she adjusted her hat in front of the mirror. She was preparing for her weekly shopping trip.

'You're in charge, Kathleen,' she said, pointing to my eldest sister. 'Would you try and keep a bit of order.'

With a quick drenching shake of holy water, my mother climbed into the trap. My father chucked the reins, sending Dolly, the mare, into a leisurely trot for the eight-mile trip to town. As the trap vanished from sight, my brother John's first thought, as usual, was of food.

'What will we cook?' he mused greedily. Butterscotch was the unanimous choice, because we knew we always had butter and sugar in the cupboard. Mrs. Beeton's cookery book wasn't much use to us if unknown and unobtainable ingredients were called for. Later, full of butterscotch, we decided it was time to fetch in the new chickens. They were soft and fluffy and in the absence of mother hen, they were all ours to pet and pamper. They picked at the breadcrumbs we scattered on the floor. Gently, they tested the saucer of water, stretching back their little yellow necks to swallow.

'Can you change the gramophone needle, John?' called Kathleen.

The gramophone! Soon we were cavorting wildly in the parlour to the scratchy strains of 'The Maid of the Sweet Brown Knowe', followed by Joe Lynch's rendition of 'The Cottage by the Lee'.

'What about the chickens?' I cried suddenly.

'Oh my God, the chickens,' gasped Kathleen. 'Give me a hand to put them back before Mam comes home.

But the kitchen was eerily empty and chickenless. We searched everywhere, under the big cupboard, behind the stairs, in the cubbyhole near the fire, but to no avail.

'Whist,' I said in alarm, 'I think I hear noises near the fire machine.'

The fire machine was a clever device, found in most old houses, which pumped air through an underground pipe that connected to the grate. It was a great help in getting the fire started but lethal if you wanted to extract small chickens from its tiny opening! We listened, ashen-faced, quieter than we'd been all day. Sure enough, we heard chirping sounds but there was no sign of a chicken.

'Oh no,' moaned Kahleen, 'I bet they've gone into the pipe.'

This was bad news. The underground pipe was completely out of our reach. Panic-stricken, we quenched the fire, sending clouds of ash, smoke and dirt sky high.

'If the pipe is hot, will the chickens get roasted?' wailed Eileen tearfully.

'Shut up, will you, and blow the machine,' snapped Kathleen.

But blowing the machine produced no results so the mother hen was next called into service.

She hesitated, standing gingerly on the hot grate but her nervous clucking brought no chicks running to her side. We noted with dismay, that the chirping noises were getting fainter and fainter.

John was no help.

''Tis all your own fault anyway. Why did you bring in the stupid chickens when you were told not to. I'm not taking any of the blame.'

We knew there was no way he would get blamed. He was the white-haired boy!

'The chirping is stopped' sobbed Eileen. We suddenly became aware of the awful silence.

'I can't take any more of this' sobbed Kathleen. 'I'm going down to the road gate to wait for them and face the music. The sooner Mam knows, the faster this terrible nightmare will be over.'

The house was a mess, the fire quenched, the chickens dead!

When my mother spotted Kathleen's white, stricken face, she feared the worst. She was sure something awful had happened to one of us. The sad fate of the chickens was trivial by comparison.

I could never blow the fire machine again without thinking of that awful day and the sad fate of the poor chickens!

WHERE'S THE LADDER?

A child longs for acceptance. In my heart I knew that this bully wasn't worth the effort but I blindly followed the others. I can still smell the chocolate and see her greedy face as she gobbled it up!

Could this plump, matronly woman, whose hand I was shaking, really be Patricia Connolly? We hadn't met in years! But I could never forget her! There's one like her in every school. You know the type. She has the most expensive leather school bag with shoulder straps, the latest pencil-case, the shiniest hair clips and the tastiest lunch. And did I mention the sharpest tongue? Yes, even just thinking about her now, almost made me insecure as the years fell away . . .

Patricia was the only girl in her family with five older brothers, and she was a spoilt brat. She gave the impression that she was slightly better than everybody else and we stupidly allowed her to believe it. It was safer to keep on the right side of her though, because you never knew what stories she would invent about your parents, your house or yourself if you didn't.

She told the tale of one family in the school that used jam pots instead of cups for drinking their tea. She said that another girl's mother was keeping a hatching hen in the bottom of the dresser in the kitchen and she delighted in relating how Margaret O'Shea had to sleep with her mother and father because their house was so tiny. How she ridiculed poor James Mulvey! He lived down a long, lonely boreen and had to walk four miles to school, often barefooted. When he contracted a bad dose of scabies she was less than sympathetic.

'It was probably the rats. I hear that their house is full of them. They must have crawled all over his face while he was asleep. I'm keeping well away from him in case I catch anything.'

Patricia must have been absent the day that the milk of human kindness was being doled out! Every day at break-time, we gathered round to see what she had brought for her lunch. The rest of us had bread and butter, and maybe a bottle of milk, but Patricia always had a bar of chocolate as well. She chewed each piece with deliberate satisfaction 'til our mouths watered! I seem to forever remember her in a blue jumper, plaid skirt with straps coming over her shoulders and brown furry boots. Her black, bushy hair was usually tied back with a red ribbon. Patricia wasn't a particularly bright student, but that in no way detracted from her power over us.

When the religious examiner came to the school, once a year, everyone wore their Sunday best. I was as proud as a peacock in my beautiful, slightly long, purple dress with tiny pink flowers on the collar and hem until Patricia Connolly looked me over critically and sniggered, 'Your mother must have got a parcel from America. You're like a scarecrow!'

Some of the other girls laughed as well until I was in tears. I never again liked the purple dress.

I was on the fringe of her entourage, and we enjoyed what I considered, an uneasy friendship. Sometimes she deigned to be almost civil to me. This made my day. However, as her temporary confidante, you were expected to be complicit in her mockery and criticism of the others, which meant that you actually ended up almost as horrible as her! I remembered how she snubbed shabbily dressed girls and refused to catch their hands when we stood around in a big circle chanting

'Wallflowers, wallflowers, growing up so high;
Me and my lady will never, never die.'

Even though she wasn't in our class, she made it clear that she was still the boss and authority on all matters. Patricia knew more about the world than we did. She told us that you got a baby from the hospital and that boys cost more than girls. She liked to fraternise with the teacher's daughter, who was allowed into her inner circle. Her mother was friendly with the Master in school and had visited his house and had seen his talking parrot. Now who could compete with that?

One Monday, at lunchtime, after she'd eaten her chocolate, while we all looked on with envy, she regaled us with her weekend news.

'We had visitors yesterday, and my cousin played the piano in the sitting-room. Mammy said that I could have lessons later on if I want. I'm delighted. I don't suppose there's a piano in your parlour, Ann?'

I could feel my face going red. How could I tell her that we certainly didn't have a piano, but that my father played the acccordion. I knew she would use this information to humiliate and belittle me. She boasted about their new wireless, and hinted that her father was thinking of buying a motorcar.

Wouldn't you wonder how any of us bothered to seek out the 'friendship' of such a spiteful little madam, but Patricia's power over us was relentless? My joy knew no bounds when my turn came to be invited to her house for a visit. My mother wondered what the big deal was as she watched me putting extra effort into my morning ablutions and picking out my nicest hair ribbon.

'I'm going to Patricia Connolly's house,' I announced proudly.

'Is that all?' smiled my mother. 'I thought you were going to see the queen. Don't be too late coming home.'

I had a great time. Her home was just an ordinary farmhouse and her mother; though a bit condescending, was nice enough. I had tea in a china cup in the parlour and I saw the piano and the wireless. We played with her doll, which was bigger and better than any doll I had ever seen. Her eyes opened and shut and she had a gorgeous white frilly dress. Patricia let me take her for a walk in the doll's pram, which I coveted with all my heart. The best part was that I had Patricia all to myself and she was almost friendly.

Now, it was my turn to ask her to my house. I looked at the place critically, trying to imagine it through Patricia's eyes. There was no point in asking my mother to start white-washing the walls as she'd only laugh at me. She was just another little girl to her, but it was make or break time for me.

My sister and I slept in the loft of our house and we loved it up there near the rafters. In order to get up or down, we used a ladder, which was hooked to the wall behind. Later on, a proper stairs was put in place. In the meantime, we were very happy with the ladder and it was very much a part of the furniture of the kitchen. Except I noticed that, when important visitors were expected, like T.D.s or Americans, my mother ordered the ladder to be taken outside. She seemed somehow, ashamed of it.

Now I, too, worried about the ladder and what Patricia would think of it. The day she was to come to my house, I was a nervous wreck. When I asked my mother if, maybe, they would consider taking out the ladder, she laughingly threw her eyes to heaven and said not to be silly. All day in school, I obsessed about the ladder. My nails were eaten down to the quick and I couldn't even enjoy Patricia's rare show of affability. Finally I took the bull by the horns.

'We have a ladder at home,' I blurted out.

'So what! No need to boast about it,' she retorted.

But I needn't have worried. When we got to my house, my mother had removed the offending ladder. She understood how important it was to me. She had also made a delicious apple tart with fresh cream from the dairy and my father played a tune on the acccordion and we danced around the kitchen laughing and singing. We nursed the new kittens on top of the hayrick. I took her to see the river and we played in my cabby-house. The visit was going well.

'Where's the famous ladder you were making all the noise about?' enquired Patricia. 'I suppose you were only making it up.'

This didn't change anything in school, of course. Patricia reverted to being her usual snotty, insulting self. You still never knew where you stood with her.

I later moved on to secondary school and quickly lost track of Patricia Connolly as I made new friends. I spread my wings and travelled away from home picking up on the news when I returned for holidays. Apparently, Patricia got a job locally in a shop and never moved outside her own parish. She was something of a social butterfly, still lording it over her friends and constantly on the look out for a suitable 'match.' Then she found a wealthy farmer, got married and reared seven children. Our paths had never crossed over the years until today.

Now, as I shook Patricia Connolly's hand, I tried in vain to reconcile her with the bossy child of my school days. She was just an ordinary, rather dull, little middle-aged woman. How on earth did I let her have such power over me? I rejoiced in the confidence maturity confers.

Patricia Connolly had lost her power.

BUTTONS AND BOWS

When the dresser is festooned with cobwebs, the floor unswept, the clock stopped and the child's hair ribbon askew you start to wonder. 'Where is the woman of the house?'

I must have been about ten years old when my mother started to feel unwell. It wasn't just an ordinary cold or flu that we all got from time to time and allowed time and nature to cure. This was different. She was irritable, anxious, had no appetite for food and suffered uncomfortable and weakening sweats. Also, more alarmingly, her eyes started to protrude. She decided to look for professional help so we knew it was serious. The doctor examined her and diagnosed a thyroid problem. He said she needed to go to hospital and have her goitre removed.

I was terribly worried. We knew about hospitals from a few years previously when my father broke his leg in a farmyard accident. He was taken to the local hospital in Clogheen, where a jolly nun, from Kerry, nursed him back to health. When his accordion was taken in to him he would play 'Kerry Long ago' for her. He was lucky. But people died in hospital.

We could see that my mother was very concerned. Dad had been lucky, all those years before, that his accident was treated in a little hospital near home. Cashel, on the other hand was a good twenty miles away and too far for Dolly, the mare to pull the trap. The only way to get there was by bus so she wouldn't be having too many visitors. I was also a little curious as to how my father would cope with the job of looking after us. My older sister was away in boarding school so at home, there was me, the youngest, my brother, who was going to the local secondary, and my other sister who was going to the nuns' school in Ballyporeen.

'How in the world will Dad look after us?' I thoughtlessly asked my mother one evening before she left. 'He doesn't know how to cook or wash and who'll tie the ribbon in my hair in the morning for school?'

My poor mother had her misgivings, too, about leaving us, but had little choice. In late spring, she packed her bag and my father accompanied her to the hospital on the bus. She was under the care of Surgeon Hogan who was reported to be an atheist

Atheists, tourists or communists all sounded equally dangerous to us. He was alleged to have said that in the hundreds of operations he carried out, he never found a soul! We thought he must be a very strange man indeed, him not being a Catholic, and wondered would my mother be safe with him at all! As it turned out, he was a wonderful surgeon and in my mother's case, at least, he did a great job. She told us afterwards that she was awake for the whole procedure and could hear the doctor and nurse talking. She had no further problems with goitre for the rest of her life.

My poor father, however, had loads of problems!

'This housekeeping is harder than I thought,' he remarked one day, as he struggled to boil the dinner and also keep an eye on the hens that were picking the whitewash off the kitchen wall. I couldn't help smiling as I watched him trying to replace a button on his Sunday shirt. Having first adjusted his glasses, he set to work. Eyes screwed up in concentration, he finally managed to guide the coarse, doubled, thread into the needle by the light of the oil lamp on the wall. He repeatedly stabbed at the small button with all his might, ensuring it wouldn't fall out again. In his lifetime!

When I asked for his help one morning before school, to tie a bow in my hair ribbon, he was 'all thumbs'.

'I'm afraid I'm as awkward at tying bows as I am at sewing on buttons,' he declared sheepishly. 'Your mother is an awful loss to us around here. That's her department.'

Anyway, I tied the ribbon myself, one piece hanging down rakishly longer than the other! The only buttons and bows my poor father knew anything about were connected to accordions and fiddles!

He fed us well. It was coming close to the month of May and we still had plenty of potatoes in the pit, onions, carrots and turnips in the shed, plus a barrel of salted bacon. The menu was more or less the same each day, but it was wholesome, healthy and plentiful. We each had our usual chores to do. Mine was to bring in straw and kindling to start the fire in the morning. My sister had to make sure that the hens and geese were secured for the night and let out and fed the following day. My brother was in charge of fetching water from the river. This was a never-ending chore.

My father always took over the lighting and maintaining of the fire, which was continuously burning in our house because we needed it for cooking. It was the heart of the home. He kept a plentiful supply of firewood, stacking the blocks high, where they dirtied the kitchen wall and knocked down all the whitewash!

Though Dad did his best, even a half-hearted attempt at fine-combing our hair, we missed the woman's touch. My mother would always have tucked us in and asked us if we were warm enough in bed. My father was more practical. He'd say, wouldn't we know enough to throw something on top of the bed if we were cold!

Despite my mother's absence, the ordinary cycle of life on the farm continued. The cows calved, the hens laid, and the latest batch of baby kittens opened their eyes to the world. Our necks and ears escaped inspection now before we went to school, but the Master made allowances because he knew that we were motherless. I felt very important when he would ask for a progress report on Mam. We knew that his wife had undergone a similar operation.

Returning from school, there was no currant cake cooling on the windowsill any more. With nobody doing the daily baking, my father had started bringing home a shop loaf from the creamery every day and we were delighted with the change.

The poor man would drape his socks, full of holes, over the fire crane, hoping somebody might take it into their heads to darn them. What a hope! 'Aren't they the quiet little socks, all the same, hanging there, not saying a word?' he'd joke. If he was trying to be subtle it was lost on us!

One night he told me a story about our cow, Judy, going to town on the bicycle and the adventures she had. I liked it because it was funny and had no moral at the end. Unlike mother's tales! His friend, Jack Gorman, called and they played music, my father on the fiddle, Jack on concertina. Jack always maintained that there was a great echo in the porch so they played out there 'til the small hours. There was no one to tell them it was time to go to bed!

One sunny Saturday morning he called us early and announced that we were going on a picnic – to THE BOG! We had one field, away from the rest of the farm, which yielded up pretty good quality turf every year. This field then, about three-quarters of a mile away, was our destination. While my father tackled up the ass and cart (an ass was more manoeuvrable in a bog), we parcelled up some bread and jam sandwiches, mugs, tea, sugar, milk and the billy can for making the tea.

Trixie, the terrier, jumped up on the cart as well and off we went. I wanted to take the cat, but Dad said her kittens needed her. As he cut the turf with the *sléan*, an implement like a bladed spade, our job was to 'foot' it. This meant stacking five or six sods of turf pyramid style to get maximum drying effect from the sun. The turf took a long time to dry but if there was a good breeze it did a good job in forming a tough, waterproof skin on the turf.

My father was an expert at turning work into play and we'd have a game to see if we could keep ahead of him with our stacking. We worked up a powerful thirst and ran over and back to the nearby stream from time to time to get mugs of water. After a few hours, we took a welcome break and he lit the fire. The billy can, full of stream water was placed on a little stone platform in the centre of the fire to boil. We took out our jam sandwiches and ate with relish. It is a well-known fact that there is no place on earth that one feels as hungry as in a bog. Sitting back, we savoured our food as though it was the nectar of the gods and Trixie waited expectantly, ears cocked, for the crusts.

We sat back in the sun, watching the butterflies and bees, the rich smell of the bog all around us. Dad told us again about his part in Ireland's struggle for independence during the Black and Tan and

Civil Wars. We shivered at the bit about his hunger strike in Portlaoise prison and how he was so weak at the end of it that he could hardly stand and had to hold on to the wall. We hated the English for what they did to him!

While we worked, Trixie kept herself amused, snapping at the big brown frogs that were plentiful in the damp undergrowth. My sister collected some tiny lizards and chased us with them. Dad kept cutting and we kept stacking as the sun sank lower in the sky. It was getting dark when we gathered our stuff together and set off for home on the ass and cart. Dad told us to wish on the first star we saw and taught us a little rhyme:

> *Star, star, shining bright*
> *First star, I've seen tonight*
> *I wish I may, I wish I might*
> *Have the wish, I wish tonight*

I wished that Mam would be well enough to come home soon from the hospital.

We got to know our father better as the days went on and heard more stories of his time in prison. He told us that he made a silver ring out of a half-crown for our mother while he was there. Because he had so much on his mind, seeing after everything, law and order around the house became relaxed.. For instance, bedtime could go unnoticed. He liked to play cards and Ludo, late into the night, so welcomed the company of any interested parties who had a few pennies to spare. I'm sure we had red eyes in the morning from want of sleep

I asked my father if I could visit Mam in hospital in Cashel, now that she was on the mend. He promised that if I won enough money for my bus fare playing Ludo with him that I could go the following day. Unfortunately luck wasn't on my side, so he went alone.

As time went on, the house took on a rather dusty, neglected look. We dodged as much as possible. After school, my father had us out on the farm, weeding turnips and helping with the cutting of the timber. Neighbours came in at night playing cards.

'I suppose you're glad she's coming back to you, Johnny?' casually remarked one of our card-players.

'Is Mam coming home?' I shrieked

'Yes,' said Dad, 'to-morrow.'

We got cracking on the kitchen and washed all the dirty dishes. John got two buckets of water and Dad went to the shop and bought a pound of sausages for the supper. He tried to make an apple tart, but it got burnt in the bastable! My sister collected all the eggs from the hen-house, washed them and put them in a bowl on the dresser and Dad made sure the fire was blazing brightly. The smoky globe around the oil lamp was cleaned.

The horse and cart was tackled up and Dad and I went up the boreen that connected to the 'top road' and waited for the bus. It wasn't the most comfortable mode of transport for somebody after an operation. But it was the best we could do.

I'll never forget how pale and weak she seemed as she climbed on to the cart. It would be late autumn before she was fully back to herself. As I sat with her on the journey home, I felt a bit strange and awkward, almost as though she was a stranger.

'Did you miss me while I was in hospital?' she asked quietly.

'I did at first, but I got used to it,' I said shyly.

'I see. I suppose that's the way it goes.'

Later, when I was in bed, I heard her telling my father what I'd said and I sensed her disappointment.

'That's children for you,' he smiled. 'You can be sure that I missed you anyway. It's great to have you home. The house was no good without you.'

'Well, it could certainly do with a good cleaning,' said Mother. I could imagine her glancing around critically at the dusty windowsills and chairs and the tapestry of cobwebs on the rafters.

'You can leave all that until you get your strength back. A bit of dust never killed anyone.' said my father philosophically.

I snuggled into my cosy bed in the loft, between my two sisters, and felt that everything was all right in my world. Mother was in charge of the buttons and bows again!

THE STATIONS

There was a time in Ireland, during the Penal Laws, when priests were on the run. They were forced to celebrate Mass at secret locations known as Mass Rocks where the local people gathered. The Stations tradition evolved from this and is a lovely old custom practised in many parishes in Ireland still. A fixed number of families are joined together and Mass is said in rotation in each house.

The priest read the station list at Sunday Mass. Molly O'Brien's name was called out for the following week. We were in Molly's station, but it wasn't our turn for another two years, much to our mother's relief!

The priest would say Mass in her home on the following Friday morning for all the members of the Station. Here, they would hand over their dues and find out who was next in line. However, it would also be an important social occasion so 70-year-old Molly would have her work cut out to try and bring the place up to scratch for the curious eyes of the neighbours. This would prove to be a very major task as Molly, who lived alone since her brother's death, kept a very messy house. The kitchen floor was always littered with boxes, bottles, bags, brushes, buckets, barrels, bushes for the fire, pots, pans and cans of paraffin oil.

The old lopsided dresser was thronged with assorted pieces of cracked china and crockery. A few dusty, willow-patterned plates, left from her mother's time, lined the top shelf and a piece of blessed palm dangled loosely from a nail. This was Molly's brand of fire insurance. The kitchen table was often covered with unwashed dishes and the mouldy remains of long-eaten dinners and mouse droppings. She just cleared a corner when she prepared the next meal. She always remembered to replenish the little oil lamp burning under the Sacred Heart picture though. Molly had her priorities right.

And so it was that the help of Tess, her neighbour, was enlisted for the big cleanup. Sure wouldn't a dab of whitewash and a lick of paint for the chairs work wonders? Tess transported all Molly's kitchen accoutrements to the shed. The unwashed delph was collected into a big tub and dispatched outside as well. These cups and saucers would be needed tomorrow after they'd had a good scrub.

The kitchen now looked strange and empty and poor Molly seemed bewildered without her 'things' around her. She made frequent trips to the shed to reassure herself that everything was still there. In the meantime, Tess was tackling the parlour, where the priest would be hearing confessions and having his breakfast. This was a spot that would come under scrutiny. The smell of must and mildew was overpowering and clouds of dust rose skywards, as Tess swept the dirty floorboards. Choking and coughing, she rushed out for air. 'A bit dusty in there, is it Tess? Sure I didn't use it since the last station, three years ago,' remarked Molly.

But the parlour was still far from station standard, so Tess forced herself to continue. In the course of her dusting operation, she lifted a cushion off one of the black stuffed parlour chairs, nearly fainting with shock. A nest of baby mice scattered to the four corners of the room.

The old gramophone had seen better days. The lid was sealed by a tangle of cobwebs. When Tess gingerly lifted the cover, she noticed a dusty record of 'The Little Old Mud Cabin' still on the turntable. Molly hadn't played it since her brother died, three years previously. It didn't seem right. When Tess stumbled on a cache of stale half-eaten biscuits behind the table, she understood why it made a desirable hideout for a mouse family.

The wind was blowing from the east on the morning of the Stations and the fire was smoking badly. The saucepan by the fire was filled with eggs, waiting to be boiled. Two neighbouring men had raised the kitchen table on top of two chairs, so now, with the white cloth and brass candlesticks, it looked like a proper altar. My brother was the server that morning and he waited importantly in his black soutane and white surplice to tend the priest.

Mrs. Carey was resplendent in her new navy costume and sank gratefully into the newly painted chair. Suspiciously, she sprang up again and was furious to realise that the red paint was only half dry.

Confessions were underway in the musty, mousy parlour. The more heavily burdened penitents preferred the dark anonymity of the confession box and stayed away, a fact that did not go unnoticed by their neighbours. By now, the kitchen was full of smoke but the priest bravely struggled through the Mass. The men nearest the door opened it wide but the coughing and spluttering continued. Tess worried about the meal laid out in the parlour – ham, bread, butter, jam, Madeira cake. Would the mice get to it first?

In spite of all the smoke, there was very little fire and it was a struggle to boil the kettle and the saucepan of eggs in the end.

'Jack, Maurice, Tom, would ye sit with Father O'Donnell for the breakfast? The women can have theirs later on.'

Mrs. Carey threw her eyes to heaven. As if things weren't bad enough already with her good costume skirt ruined, and her stomach rumbling with the hunger. However, women knew the rules. It was important to provide respectable male company for the priest while he was eating. Females at the table would be an embarrassment and a distraction.

Halfway through the Mass, my brother, the erstwhile altar boy, decided that discretion was the better part of valour and went home. He told my mortified parents that the smoke was too much for him. When my father later apologised for his desertion, the priest laughed and said he was put to the pin of his collar to finish the Mass himself.

The smoke still hung over the kitchen, but Molly didn't mind. She was well used to that. Now, that everybody had gone, she turned to Tess with a sigh of relief, 'Didn't that go well now, but thank God it's over. Maybe you'd give me a hand to bring in my stuff out of the shed. I miss my things around me and that's the truth. The house is queer and lonesome without them.'

And so Molly's kitchen returned to its old untidy self again. There wouldn't be any need to clean it again until the next Station in three years time!

THE GAMBLE

I ran excitedly from the kitchen to the parlour and back again so as not to miss any of the preparations. The fires were lit. The tables were ready. The stools and chairs were lined up by the back wall. The keg of porter was waiting to be uncorked ...

'I think we'll have a gamble on Friday night!' My mother's knitting needles clicked and glinted in the firelight as she glanced cautiously around to gauge the reaction to her announcement. If there was one thing my father loved more than anything it was playing cards so the prospect of a gamble was music to his ears. I was over the moon, of course, immediately conjuring up the houseful of neighbours, cake and lemonade, confusion and excitement when maternal supervision would be slack. With any luck, bedtime might go unnoticed!

Card playing was the favourite pastime in many houses in the forties and fifties and ours was no exception. The stakes were small, perhaps twopence a game with a few sixpenny rubbers towards the end of the night. A gamble was different. The grand prize for the winner might be either a goose or a turkey. My father told me he once played for a goat. There was a story about the same animal. Apparently, each person who won it, put it up for gamble again and it was only after a couple of months, when somebody finally decided to collect his prize that the goat was found to be dead!

Gambles took place in the winter, when farm work was slack and diversion badly needed to dispel the gloom of bitter weather and short days. Since my mother always had a flock of geese at hand, we had the prize ready at all times.

'Clear out of the kitchen, out of my way let ye, so I can wash the floor!' ordered Mother.

Although it was winter, and the floor would take ages to dry, my mother got busy with her scrubbing brush and basin of water. Soon, the cement glistened wetly. It was Friday morning and she had to have the place spick and span for the gamble. Towards evening, she placed the newly scrubbed wooden table in front of the window. The paraffin lamp (taken from its customary spot near the fire) was positioned overhead to afford maximum light. My father was all business, gathering a great pile of wood. The big block for the back of the fire was very important as it threw out enough heat to warm the entire kitchen.

The keg of porter sat importantly on the parlour floor, supervised by a dear friend, with a delightful, quirky sense of fun. He could be described as a 'character', a once off type of individual, of which rural Ireland had a rich pool in those days. He also had an unfortunate weakness for the drink, so putting him in charge of the porter was like leaving a fox minding a hen! He dispensed the refreshment judiciously so it would last the night. Everybody was too engrossed to notice his steady deterioration as the gamble progressed, though his customary repartee never faltered!

We revelled in the strangeness of a lit-up parlour, where the table was laid out with cups, saucers and plates of sweet cake. The sideboard mirror gleamed in the light from the crackling wood fire and our eyes shone with excitement. We held our breath in anticipation. This time, just before the neighbours gathered in, was perhaps the best moment of all . . .

News of the gamble was spread by word of mouth, often by the creamery-goers, and we always had a full house. People would start to arrive about 8 p.m. except for one old lady, who would come around 6.30 p.m. She was on time for the rosary and a comfortable seat by the fire. She was only there for the dancing, but still contributed her few shillings. Somebody else played for her.

'Forty-five' was the game, with six people to each table. Knaves were cast to decide on partners, who then sat opposite each other. Occasionally 'nines' were played but this was difficult to count. Some people were known for making 'tokens' to their partners but my father frowned on this custom. (Playing tokens is where partners make nods and gestures to each other to indicate what cards they are holding, which would give them an unfair advantage.)

I seem to remember that the men almost had a monopoly when it came to playing cards. Women weren't yet liberated. The exchanges back and forth were intriguing. There was much disputing about the play, the count, who reneged from the five or who hit the low man. The finer points of the game were lost on me. However. I couldn't fail to get excited when someone would hit the table an almighty wallop, sending the cards dancing, and produce the ace of hearts on the last day when everybody thought the game was gone. God help the one who let the game slip through careless play.

My father often told the story of a good friend and neighbour who was playing in the final of one of our gambles. The prize was a kid goat and his partner, a seriously dedicated card player, badly wanted that goat. As luck would have it, they got to as far as the very last game and were thirty-five for out. Our friend, who was more interested in music than cards, heard my father playing the accordion in the parlour and he momentarily lost his concentration. He had the five of trumps in his hand but forgot to play it and somebody else got there before him and won the goat. He quickly hid the five. His partner would surely have killed him if he ever found out!

Our gambles had a double attraction. Those who didn't want to play cards retired to the parlour for lemonade and the dance and this was my opportunity to scrutinise the style and make-up of the ladies. These local girls, with their red-painted mouths and ghost-like powdered faces were as near as I'd got, so far, to a film star. I had less interest in the well-scrubbed, oily-haired neighbouring boys who were watching the ladies closely, ready to pounce, like a cat after a mouse, when my father struck up a waltz. I was trying to interpret the nods and winks passing back and forth between them. The keeper of the barrel was becoming a bit wobbly, but still standing.

Tea was passed around to the players and dancers. The going was hot and heavy now. The dancers and gamblers changed rooms.

Those who were still in the play for the goose were dispatched to the parlour to finish the game while the newly washed cement floor in the kitchen resounded to the hob-nailed boots and shouts of 'Mind the dresser!' My father played 'The Blackbird' and 'Miss McLeod's Reel' with spirit and gusto. Half-sets and waltzes followed in quick succession, the bystanders shouting words of encouragement

'No bother to you, Maggie!' or 'Don't stand on her toes, James!'

Sometimes I would coax Trixie the dog, on to the floor as I didn't want him to lose out on the fun. The desperate look in the poor animal's eyes, as she balanced precariously on her hind legs, shattered any illusions I might have that she was enjoying the dance. My mother might unwittingly, come to her rescue shouting, 'Will someone put out that dog!'

She found a partner for the patient lady beside the fire and this made her night. She was sometimes prevailed upon to sing, which, I'm afraid, was a great source of amusement to us in those irreverent childhood days. I got an update on the progress of the courting couples that had got as far as the porch. Later, the door opened and they quietly disappeared into the night. It was very romantic. I wanted them to get married and live happily ever after.

The last dregs of porter were drained from the barrel and its keeper staggered home, singing softly to himself. The victorious gambler, departed proudly, with his goose slung over his shoulder in a brown bag. The goose might be further fattened up in time to grace their Christmas table.

A gamble could last all night. After the goose was won, neighbours often played rubbers. I once remember watching the dawn breaking while the strains of music and merriment continued unabated in the house. A neighbour would remind my father of the night that 'the prime boys' threw the red pepper down our chimney during a gamble. The noxious fumes scattered the crowd as they ran spluttering and coughing into the yard!

When everybody had finally left, we crept out of bed and sat in the corner with our parents by the dying embers of the fire, the big block now reduced to a heap of white ash. We recounted every little detail of the night again. 'Did you see the way Mossie kept an eye to the barrel?' 'Did you see the tokens between Jim and Mick?' 'Wasn't Josie, back from England, looking great?'

'Did Katie Murphy dance at all?' my mother wondered.

' Sure she hadn't time', laughed my father. 'Did you see the amount of talk she was putting out of her. She hardly drew breath. I spotted her licking her lips one time like she was putting up edge!' (My father was comparing her action to the edging of a saw before cutting wood in order to improve performance!)

'She enjoyed herself anyway. That's the main thing,' said my mother, smothering a yawn.

And so it went on. Our eyes were closing with the sleep. We were so happy that our gamble was a success. It would be the main topic for discussion at the creamery next morning.

GOING TO THE CREAMERY

This was a vital daily farm procedure as people were very dependent on their creamery cheques. Only a bad farmer was late for the Creamery. It was almost as bad as being late for Mass!

I have an abiding memory of riding to school, on the back of the old creamery cart. This was drawn by Dolly, our beloved white mare. How I enjoyed watching the tarred road disappearing beneath my dangling feet, which would be spared the two-mile walk for once. If I'd made the effort, I could have availed of this lift every morning and been on time for school! However, the lad who was driving the cart delighted in giving me the slip.

In those far-off days, going to the creamery was undoubtedly the most important daily task. Collecting and straining the milk and filling the scalded churns were all part of the laborious preparations.

The other possibilities of the milk churns were also explored. I liked the nice echo effect I got when I stuck my head into the mouth of the churn and did my Bridie Gallagher impersonation.

My father built a stand in the front yard under a large shady tree to facilitate the manoeuvring of the churns on to the cart. Beside it was a water trough, into which the churns were dropped, to keep the milk cool.

Donkey and cart, or horse and cart were the mode of transport to the creamery and you could tell a farmer's financial standing by the number of churns. On arrival at the creamery (which in our case was Kilbehenny) the farmers lined up in an orderly queue. They chatted to their neighbours while they waited. Even the animals turned their heads and played whickering and snorting games with each other.

When your turn came the creamery assistant lifted in and weighed the 'new milk' and replaced it in the churn with 'back milk'. This skimmed milk was a great boon to my father for feeding calves and pigs and it also had its uses in the kitchen.

Women rarely took the milk to the creamery. It was considered a man's job and if a husband was sick, a charitable neighbour would usually step into the breach. Only a very brave, or forward, woman would chance going into this male dominated arena, unless she didn't mind being the talk of the parish!

The creamery book was sacred and carefully minded. It was handed in each morning to the creamery manager – a god-like creature who was addressed as 'Sir'! He recorded the number of gallons of milk received and the amount of butter and animal feed given out. It was like a transaction card. Ours had a green cover and was kept on the front window of the kitchen. Once, as a child, I dared to scribble with a black crayon on its grainy whiteness. The manager was not amused and when he questioned this violation I got a telling-off from my father. The monthly creamery cheque was eagerly awaited and kept us ticking over.

This, more or less, constituted the official creamery business. But there was the equally important social side to consider. Here was a glorious opportunity to exchange ideas and gossip with your neighbour. All human life was discussed, from politics, distant world events to salacious local scandals. Stories, rumours, exaggeration, innuendo, scheming and double dealings were all grist to the mill. Weddings, funerals, christenings and murders were discussed and pondered over. Sheep and cattle prices were debated.

You got to hear of upcoming events like gambles, threshings, pioneer excursions to Tramore and pilgrimages to Knock. Free legal aid was generously dispensed at the creamery regarding trespassing and rights of way. You could get information on where to locate a reliable thatcher, a good bottle of poteen or a young gander. Some farmers also purchased household commodities at the local shop before returning home to a welcoming cup of tea and a wife agog with curiosity for all the latest news.

It was no mean task to have the milk ready and on time for the creamery each morning. My parents would be up very early during the summer months, milking the cows and regulating the milk. We had a young lad helping on the farm who 'did' the creamery. One morning he overslept and rushed madly to be on time. About a mile from Kilbehenny, he tied the donkey to a bush and ran the rest of the way to the village to see if the creamery was still open!

Going to the creamery
(photograph courtesy of Avondhu Paper)

My father had another story. A neighbour of ours had an extremely well-trained donkey that managed the creamery on its own. The farmer loaded up the cart, pointed the ass in the direction of the creamery and off it went. It stood in line with the other horses and carts and when the man in charge had completed the business, he turned the animal for home, gave him a slap on the backside and it trotted back to his own yard.

In later years, tractors and trailers and motorcars were used for transporting milk as donkeys and horses passed into history. Farming methods became revolutionised and updated beyond recognition. These days milk is collected from the farms by a motorised 'bulk tank'. This sounded the death knell for many small farmers who could no longer compete with stringent testing, milk coolers, quotas and red tape.

When we were growing up we thought creameries were there for good. We could never imagine that such a vital facet of country life, with all the attendant fun and social interaction, would, like so many other things, become a victim of progress.

GOING TO MASS

God and De Valera were the two important men in our house when I was a child. Being a Catholic and Fianna Fail, I felt we were on the right track. Going to Sunday Mass was a given and not up for discussion unless you were at death's door!

I know church attendance is not as popular nowadays, especially among young people. But when I was a girl going to Mass on Sunday was central to our lives. It was almost like a barometer of the state of your health.

'Is she back at Mass yet?' You might hear somebody ask.

My mother always maintained that Sunday was odd in some way if you didn't fulfil your weekly obligation. Sure, didn't Mass keep you in touch with God, your neighbours and parish events? It set you up for the week. Religious fervour wasn't always the main reason for going either. Since ladies kept their heads covered in church, here was a chance to shine. Mightn't some strapping local lad fall under the spell of your hat as you made your way up the aisle?

''Tis all the clocks – go out and listen for carts on the road, let ye!' cried my mother anxiously.

Our clock was often slow. If you got in to Mass after the Gospel was read you were considered late and had a mortal sin chalked up against you. Mortal sins could qualify you for hell! Confusion reigned as everybody rushed around the kitchen.

'Where's my clean shirt?' yelled my brother.

He grabbed something white that was airing before the fire. He always assumed that items being aired were meant for him. God forbid that the '*buachaillín fionn*' would get a cold in his kidneys from wearing something damp!

'Would you give me that!' shouted my sister indignantly. 'My new angora jumper! Wouldn't it be in a nice state after you?

My father was quietly working up a lather of foam with his shaving brush at the little dresser. Mother was trying to straighten her stockings and her hat at the same time and I was hopping impatiently from one foot to the other wondering who was going to tie my hair ribbon.

'Johnny, would you scatter the fire. Lads, don't forget your rosary beads and get a bottle for holy water.'

Dolly, the old reliable white mare, had been put in the paddock near the house the previous evening so she was caught without too much trouble. Now, she was tackled to the trap, waiting to transport us to church. She shed her white hairs with abandon as she trotted along, so we always brought a clothes brush! A watchful eye was kept also for any twitching or arching of her tail. The last thing we needed was a lump of horse dung landing on our good Sunday clothes! We saluted our neighbours in their horses and traps, relieved that we were in good time. Dolly was tied in a neighbour's yard and we took our accustomed places in the silent, dim chapel.

Women and children usually sat on the left hand side, while the men stayed on the right. Some old timers stayed in the porch or even outside the door, kneeling meditatively on their cap on one knee, ready for a quick get-away. The older women in the back pew had their heads together, whispering about clocking hens, egg prices and local scandals. The newly married woman, walking up the aisle, who'd put on a bit of weight, came under their scrutiny. They counted months on their fingers.

As I waited for Mass to start, I took stock of the different hats and headscarves. The blue lakes of Killarney rippled down the side of Mrs McGrath's head and I ducked sideways to catch the changing view when she bowed. Mrs English's autumnal scarf was a blaze of reds and oranges and Joan Muldoon's had a picture of the grotto in Lourdes. I darted a quick, frightened glance at Mrs. Molloy's fox-fur, paws still attached, glittering vixen eyes staring glassily!

'Introibo ad altare Dei,' intoned the priest solemnly.

'Ad Deum qui laetificat, juventutum meam,' returned the black and white altar boys, quick as lightning! The priest had his back turned to us and continued with his Latin prayers. My sister was sure that he made them up as he went along. We got out our rosary beads, trying not to fidget or look around.

After the solemn moment of consecration, there was a palpable sigh from the congregation and coughs that had been manfully suppressed, got full expression. I always recognised my father's cough! The Sunday sermon gave guidelines on staying out of Hell. They regularly focused on company keeping and occasions of sin. The self-righteous older generation sat smugly, as they felt that it had nothing to do with them. The young ones squirmed uncomfortably in their seats!

In those pre-television times, when the missioner came for a week he gave great entertainment and was assured of a packed church each night. Missioners, especially the Redemptorists, were experts at putting the fear of God into you. They had especially well-developed lungs and their roars could be heard for miles. They got the parishioners back on the straight and narrow. People were passionately penitent. On the last evening, our missioner was doing his final routine with the renewal of the baptismal vows.

'Do you renounce the devil?' he roared

'We do!' answered the crowd

'With all his works and pomps ...'

One over-zealous member of the congregation got carried away and shouted louder than the rest

'We do, the hoor!'

After a mission, people did a spiritual spring clean. Neighbours fixed their differences and longstanding bills in shops were paid. A few unfortunate souls however took the mission too much to heart and ended up in the mental hospital for a spell.

At Communion, which was at the very end of Mass, the priest placed the host on your tongue. 'Corpus Cristi', he murmured. You would swallow reverently as you had been told, not letting your teeth touch the sacred host. That was such a delicate manoeuvre that you would nearly choke. Receiving Holy Communion was usually a monthly event and very careful preparation was made with lengthy prayers, before and after.

Sometimes, we had a long cold wait in the trap, while father, who was a member of the County Council, dealt with various problems regarding roads, bridges or housing. The good lady, in whose yard Dolly was tied, often brought us in for tea. We might end up staying half the day!

The well-off parishioner always seemed to be more in favour with the clergy. The story goes of one particular priest meeting the local businessman who lived down the street. As he went into Mass, with his umbrella, on a particularly wet Sunday morning, the priest greeted him warmly saying, 'Well aren't you the great man, to be going to Mass on such a bad day.'

But there was no word of welcome for the poor peasant farmer, with no umbrella, who had walked from the top of the Galtees, drowned to the skin.

When I was in boarding school, we were expected to attend daily Mass, unless you were at death's door and then you got castor oil! We became very devout, saying little aspirations from a special booklet at lunch-time when we visited the church. Every class began with a prayer. I began to get hooked on all the rituals and actually missed going to Mass when I went home on holidays. My mother was sure I had a vocation.

Sr. Declan, a much-loved teacher, had great devotion to the Mass. In her weekly pep talks to us on Saturday nights, she always urged us to make it part of our lives.

What would she think of us today? Did she ever think she'd see the priest facing the congregation with his back to the tabernacle? How could she have envisaged Latin being replaced by English, the advent of Saturday night Mass, the level of lay participation in the ministry; or little girls serving the priest? So much has changed. Women now go hatless and are no longer bothered by how they dress in church. Many people consider that it's no longer a sin to miss Mass on Sunday. And some youngsters don't consider that anything's a sin! There are no more hard-hitting sermons at Mass on occasions of sin and company-keeping. Their words would fall on deaf ears! We were remarking on this lately and an elderly friend of mine, after considering the change in the times declared, somewhat regretfully I thought, 'Well, if all them things aren't sins any more, aren't we after missing the world of shport!'.

SAVING THE HAY

We have a faded picture, taken on the old Brownie camera of haymakers leaning on their pike handles, smiling at the sun. They all had their braces pulled down over their shoulders, shirtsleeves pulled up to the elbows. Maybe it was a Sunday (and a special dispensation had been given for bad weather) because one man had a collar and tie on!

Haymaking conjures up gloriously sunny days, which seemed to come often in the long ago summers of my childhood. But were they always sunny?

'I heard the call of the corncrake to-day,' remarked my father one evening at the supper. 'It's a reminder that we'd want to be thinking about cutting the hay. I hope to God we get a few fine days.'

My mother put a special trimming into the rosary for good weather. Sometimes the priest included it in the prayers at Mass as well. Farmers could do many a job in the rain but saving hay was definitely not one of them.

Dad would start by cutting a few swathes of hay around by the headland of the field to make a passage for the hay-machine. Being a most methodical worker, he attended to each part of the preparation with meticulous attention. This drove us mad. We wanted to go out there and get dug in straight away! When the hay was finally cut, it was vital that we got a bit of sun to save it. If luck was on our side, we might awake to a cloudless blue sky and our hearts would be gladdened to see one or two kindly neighbours arriving with pikes over their shoulders, ready to lend a helping hand.

Before long, the hayfield would be a hive of activity and friendly banter, as the new mown hay was tossed and turned, caressed by the breeze and dried by the warm sun. I would sometimes help my mother to prepare the tea, which was taken out to the hayfield, together with slices of buttered, home-made currant cake. There was a relaxed feeling, as we sat down to enjoy a well-earned rest.

My father maintained that tea always tasted better in the hayfield, despite the fact that dust and insects might fall into your cup! Nothing could take away from our simple enjoyment of this impromptu picnic. We lay back against the warm cocks of hay, letting the sunds of birds and insects and the sweet heady smell of the meadow wash over us. Sometimes, we scattered in terror as a big green frog with bulging eyes, hopped up beside us, but Sally, the dog, sent him flying!

This was the time for lively conversation about local and current events. Invariably, my father re-told the old stories of his experiences during the Black and Tan and Civil Wars. He was sent to Dublin on the train with a dispatch one time. What better place to hide a document than in the bellows of his accordion which he had with him. As luck would have it, who was he sharing the compartment on the train with him but two Black and Tan soldiers?

'Play a tune for us, Paddy,' they laughed. And my father entertained the two men all the way to Dublin! He was a born storyteller and was never in a hurry to get back to the hay-making. My father had a different work philosophy to most other farmers we knew. He was never impatient to get a job finished. He appreciated nature and was content to work with it, turning a hard task into a sort of game, in which we children, unwittingly participated.

However, we now had a job to finish A few days previously after the hay had dried it had been gathered into small cocked heaps. Now it was ready for the final exercise in haymaking. The cocks were assembled to make fewer, but much larger wynds or 'trams'. Pikeful after pikeful was hoisted aloft until a well-proportioned dome of hay stood before us. My sister sometimes got the job of standing on top to prevent the wynd rising up too quickly.

A *sugán* rope was tied lengthways and crossways to secure each wynd from wind and weather. I had made these *sugáns* earlier with father. From a bundle beside him, he would draw out lengths of hay, which I would turn with a little gadget called a twister. When the required length was reached, my father would roll each *sugán* into a whiskery ball, ready for use. Any leftover balls of *sugán* were used to put new seats on our kitchen chairs. You needed strong hands for this job and it fell to us to trim off the stray wisps with the scissors.

Haymaking scene

Pulling the butts of the wynds was a job mostly assigned to the younger members of the family, who were considered more agile for bending down but it was an unenviable job as the nettles and thistles stung your hands. It was to prevent the grass from closing up around the bottom of the wynd, making it easier later on to attach a rope around it when it was being swung into the hay-barn by Dolly the white mare. This procedure was also called 'sligging' in parts of the country. If you were really posh, you might own a hay car or bogey. My sister and I also got the job of raking up the last stray bundles of hay scattered around the field before the ass and cart transported it into the barn with the rest.

The hay, however, was left to mature in the fields for some weeks before being taken in. We loved this part, since we weren't expected to get involved in the work, so we could enjoy the fun. We would steal a ride at the back of the wynd, as it was being swung in from the field, hanging on very tightly. We often dislodged big bundles of hay, which left us marooned on the ground, while Dolly continued on her merry way! It must have been a satisfying moment for my father when all the crop was safely tucked away in the barn and winter feed for the livestock was assured for another year.

The hay-barn was supposed to be off-limits to us, because of the danger of falling off the long ladder, which reached to the top of the rick. Of course, that never stopped us! Also, my father didn't want us to be knocking down the hay as we wriggled and dived into its comforting softness. Here was insulation from worry and care, and mother's voice, calling you to do jobs. It was a good place to take a friend, cuddle a new pup or recite your favourite rhymes. I believe that hay-barns were often used for romantic assignations as well! Nowadays, the laborious task of saving the hay has been revolutionised by highly technical machinery, which can be operated by one man. My brown faded photograph of a smiling group of pike-wielding hay-makers, is all I have left to remind me that those other happy days really did exist.

PLAY ACTING

When I was in Dublin in the sixties, going to the theatre was considered a posh thing to do. However, country people like me made no great wonder of it. Weren't we well used to shows and plays? The Abbey was just an extension of the village hall!

Children are natural play actors from the time they're born. When little girls play with their dolls they really live the part. It's the same with boys playing cowboys and Indians.

So it was with me! When I was six or seven I threw my casting director's eye around the farmyard for a suitable 'baby' for my cabby-house. I picked a tame, half-reared cat and dressed him up in a doll's dress and hat and put him lying on his back in a box. The tail was a bit of a problem. The whiskery face could be hidden with the bonnet, but the tail stuck out. Now everybody knows that lying on its back is not a natural position for a cat, so I had to use a lot of persuasion – and pressure – to hold him. Still, when my back was turned for a second, he would streak like a shot out of the box, protesting loudly, and by the time I got him down from the tree, the doll's clothes were in tatters!

My brother gave us parts in the plays, which he wrote himself, and cast us according to our ages and height. I remember one in particular, because it contained the chilling line, 'Get the pan to hold the blood!'

Dad would spend a few hours hammering old planks together to create a makeshift stage. My mother, having turned down folds in two old sheets and threaded a length of twine through them, tied one end to a nail near the front window and the other to the cupboard on the other side. After all, what's a play without curtains! The stage was positioned in front of a small bedroom, which acted as our dressing-room, so now everything was perfect. The glow from the oil lamp on the kitchen wall and the flying sparks from the big open fire created the atmosphere as a few elderly neighbours, along with our parents, indulgently cheered us on. I was a leprechaun in an upside-down redundant playpen once and had no lines at all to say. Maybe I couldn't talk! My big crime was that I ate the sweets intended for the raffle!

In the summer time we took our plays outside to the pig house and spent many happy hours in our make-believe world.

When my sisters, Kathleen and Eileen, went to Ballyporeen school for a year after their primary, and before they started secondary, the nuns included them in their famous St. Patrick's night concerts. These were magical. My mother and I were so proud, sitting in the audience, while my sisters went through their paces. The girls' costumes were made from green crepe paper, made by the parents and nuns. The little boys had black pants, white shirts and dickey bows! They looked gorgeous. They performed funny sketches, songs and delightful dance routines. I loved the slow elegant dance called the 'gavotte' executed with grace and style by a tiny, serious little boy and his partner. My sister Kathleen had a minor part in one of the sketches called 'Mary Ellen' and we, subsequently, learned it all off and would perform it relentlessly when visitors came!

Then there were the travelling plays or 'fit ups'. These were talented, travelling players who had yet to find a home in famous theatres, such as the Abbey. Usually, one of their members would come to the school and the teacher would allow him to tell the children about their up-coming productions. I would race home from school, breathless with excitement.

'Mam, Mam, there's a play in the hall tomorrow night. Can I go, please, please, please.'

'We'll see,' was my mother's usual answer, but I knew it was a done deal. She loved the plays as much as I did.

The organisers had 'forums' or long wooden planks arranged to accommodate the crowd. We waited, hardly daring to breathe, for the curtains to part. We had got glimpses of actors darting behind the stage in strange costumes and couldn't wait. The hall was packed with parents and children and people from the neighbouring parishes. Then, a hush came on the crowd as the curtains were slowly pulled back and the play started. On stage, an old lady with a black shawl sat on a chair crying, and wringing her hands

'Ochón is Ochón ó,' she wept. 'Will I ever see my Joseph again?'

We all waited and wept with her, spellbound, as the story unfolded. It was called 'Pal of my Cradle Days' and told the story of a son who'd gone to the bad in England and lost his faith. We breathed a sigh of relief when he was re-united with his aging mother in the end. It was both happy and sad and we were exalted and exhausted with the suspense of it all! We lived through the drama and I even noticed a tear in my mother's eye at the end.

'We'll be lucky if we don't get our death of cold from those old forums. I'd swear they're pure damp,' declared my mother, coming sharply back to earth as she rubbed the back of her coat suspiciously. Sure enough, she got a dose of cold afterwards and swore she'd never go again. But she did!

The fun wasn't over yet. When the play finished the local accordion player started up. When he got tired the play crowd had records of pop songs. We all danced and had a great time. We saw the old lady who'd played the part of the mother in the play. Wasn't she just a young girl with a head of blonde curls on her and not a tear in sight! We walked the two miles home afterwards, but never noticed the journey as we went over every bit of the play again.

I think a bit of play-acting would be good for us at any age. What could be better than getting away from ones own mundane selves and into somebody else's skin for a few hours!

PARCELS FROM AMERICA

These parcels injected a bit of much-needed magic into the normal routine of our lives, as we danced around the kitchen with a silky dress belonging to Aunt Ciss trailing around our ankles!

Being the youngest of three girls I wore a lot of hand-me-downs when I was a child. Sometimes, as well, Mother used her creativity to add to my wardrobe. One year, I remember, it was the fashion to insert a contrasting colour in your coat to lengthen it when it got too short. She did a great job of putting a piece of black velvet into my red coat and I wore it with great pride. But even if you had the money and the transport, the local shops were very limited in their clothing choices anyway, so everyone was in the same boat, fashionwise! Clothes were functional. They were for keeping out the rain and chill, because people spent more time outdoors then. But even the insides of houses could be very cold in the winter. There was rising damp and draughts everywhere.

My mother knitted us warm woollen jumpers and stockings. These were held up with elastic garters, which left a big red marks on your legs! Mother liked nice 'style' herself and at one stage, I can remember her wearing a navy costume going to Mass with a pair of matching court shoes. She also had several hats, which she stored in hatboxes, in the parlour. I wished that she would wear lipstick, though I don't think that my father would have been too impressed! Women and children only got a new coat every few years so it was well-minded. The colours available at that time were woefully drab: bottle green, navy blue and 'nigger' brown! Imagine asking for this colour today!

Of course, it was unheard of for females to wear trousers, so it was dresses or skirts at all times. In the summer, I wore a light cotton dress and cardigan and canvas shoes that were as light as a feather. I could fly around the fields like a butterfly. Every Saturday night I applied whitening cream and placed them outside on the windowsill to dry. They would be sparkling white for Mass on Sunday. That's if the flies didn't stick to them! By September, they would be worn out and threadbare and it would be back to stout, sturdy, winter shoes again.

Wellington boots were the popular choice of footwear for farmers' families, including the wives. Even though they were smelly and uncomfortable, it was the only way to keep dry, working on the land, where you were surrounded by cow-dung and muck. A layer of newspaper under the socks helped to keep the feet warm and absorb the sweat. The woman of the house would shout to her man coming in for the night, 'For God's sake, would you leave those dirty Wellingtons outside the door and not be bringing muck and puddle onto my newly-scrubbed floor!'

But many a man sneaked in with the Wellingtons still on and, as he sat by the fire, a pungent, steamy smell of manure, sweat and the stench of burning rubber, would rise up around him!

Going to school we wore good, strong, usually black, shoes and my father would repair them in the work-shop as necessary. Dad kept his good navy suit for Sundays and special outings. A tailor in Ballyporeen, called Jim Hennessy made it for him. When it got worn out and shiny from wear it was relegated to use around the farm. My brother wore short pants until he was about thirteen. When he graduated to the long ones it signalled a right of passage. He was a man now.

The only time we were really worried about new clothes was coming up to the day of the Religious Examination in school. God help the child who didn't come in with something different. My mother always managed to find us something new. The religious examiner didn't notice what we wore at all.

Can you imagine then, the excitement that a parcel from America might generate! We probably only ever got three or four but it seemed like they came regularly.

Three members of my father's family emigrated to America in the early part of the twentieth century. However, it was mostly Aunt Ciss who sent us the parcels. She had also posted us pictures of the family over the years. There were three children, one boy and two girls, in smart clothes with straight, white teeth and smiling, American faces.

We passed our postman's house on our way back from school every day. When he had something big, he'd watch out for us, saying, 'I've a parcel for ye and it's too heavy for the bike. Tell your father to come up.'

We'd race home from school, breathless with excitement.

'Dad, tackle the horse quick. Maurice said there's a parcel and you have to collect it straight away. We'll go with you. Hurry up!'

There was no thought of a supper that evening. When we finally had the big brown box sitting on the kitchen table, we were light-headed with anticipation.

'Get the scissors out of the cupboard, quick,' ordered my mother impatiently.

'One minute,' said my father, adjusting his glasses on top of his nose. 'Take it easy now. I'll open the cords. They might come in handy again.'

Would he ever get a move on! I was hopping from one leg to the other, wondering when would I see the inside of the parcel We were all standing in a semi-circle, our eyes riveted on the box on the table, but my father would not be rushed.

He was tantalisingly slow, examining the labels and the date the parcel was sent and noting my aunt's return address on the back.

'Don't all them Yanks have the same old scrawl' he observed to my mother as he traced his sister's sloping handwriting. 'Isn't it terrible engineering all the same though, when you think about it, that this parcel is after crossing the Atlantic sea and it's after arriving into our kitchen dry and safe.'

'Johnny, would you hurry up for God's sake! We'll cut that last bit of twine. Here, give it to me.'

'Hold on a minute now. I nearly have it.'

My father had finally managed to untie all the knots and now he was rolling up the twine. He slowly, methodically, proceeded to pull back the cardboard flaps to reveal, at last, the Pandora's box of treasures! Now, he sat by the fire and lit a cigarette as we tore into the box.

'Ciss must have put on weight,' said my mother, squinting, at a big wide shapeless garment she was holding up to the light of the window. 'Still we might be able to make a pair of curtains for John's room out of it. It's a nice enough pattern.'

'Oh, can I have this, please, please,' I pleaded, as I pulled out a brightly coloured shawl, holding it up to my face. It had the smell of America and would be great for dressing up for plays.

My aunt's children were considerably older than us so their clothes didn't fit. My sister, Kathleen, had spotted a green suit that might do her after my mother had made some alterations. She liked any colour that wasn't navy – the colour of her school uniform!

'What's this?' said my mother, holding up a package labelled 'candy and cookies for the kids'.

'What are candies and cookies?' I asked.

'Ah, that's just another name for biscuits and sweets,' replied my mother.

'Please Mam, don't give them to the goat,' I begged.

'What do you mean? Oh, come on,' laughed my mother. 'Sure, don't they call children kids in America'?

It seemed I had a lot to learn! The sweets and biscuits tasted a bit different but that didn't stop us from making short work of them! We weren't fussy.

There was a light blue jacket that my aunt thought would suit my brother, now that he was a teenager. John, a shy boy, said he wouldn't be caught dead in it. Wouldn't the boys in school have a great laugh. My mother decided she'd stuff a cushion with it. My father got an emerald green tweed cap. He smilingly said he could wear it going to Mass on St. Patrick's day. There were a couple of 'sweaters' that fitted my mother.

'Isn't there very light stuff in them, Johnny?' she commented to my father as she rubbed the synthetic material between her fingers. 'Of course, they don't be out in the weather over there.'

'They wouldn't be a lot of use feeding the calves on a cold winter's morning, right enough. Couldn't you put two on together!' smiled my father. 'Sure everyone knows that Yanks are pure daft, but wasn't it good of Ciss to remember us all the same?'

Eileen pounced on some comics, wondering were they like our own. She tried on what looked like a long coat with a tassle tying it around the middle.

'That's a dressing gown,' said my mother, who knew about those things. 'That will come in handy later on for one of you.'

One time, Eileen and I got matching 'fur coats'. They were light brown with colourful decorations down the front where the buttons tied. They were warm and cosy and we wore them for years. We would all find something, whether it fitted or not. The more impractical and unsuitable the items, the better we liked them. They represented another world of bright colours, careless indulgence and sunshine. I made up my mind that I would go to America, when I was big, to see my aunt and cousins and tell them how their parcels had brightened up our lives.

Oh, but I'd have to learn to talk American first!

CURTAINS FOR THE PIG

When we saw our friend William arriving on his bicycle with an ominous brown bag on the carrier, we were worried. He was taken to the execution chamber and proceeded to roll up his sleeves. The huge knife, its flashing blade glinting in the light, was removed from the bag. This was my cue to run away – far away. But I could still hear the pig's dying roar.

Farm animals played a huge part in our childhood. Unlike today, we all lived together in close proximity and they became like our extended family. We always enjoyed the bold antics of our pig, as he snorted, grunted and rooted his way around the farmyard, covered in muck. In fact, the dirtier he got, the better pleased he seemed to be. I loved to watch him eating. He had no manners at all and would extract the last ounce of pleasure from his food as he chewed greedily and noisily.

My father would often rear a sow who would, in time, have a litter of bonhams. It was common in those days for a farmer, or one of the family, to stay up all night when the sow was having her babies. There was a danger that she would lie on them or even that she might eat one. Therefore, it was important that the job was supervised and there was no shortage of volunteers here. Staying up all night sounded very exciting. But we discovered after a few hours that it wasn't all that it was cracked up to be. Weak bonhams were brought in and placed in front of the fire. A sow could have a dozen babies so after all the others were sold off, one would be kept for fattening.

This pig had a very varied diet. Small potatoes would be boiled in a big pot over the fire for his dinner. There were also scraps from the kitchen, mash, windfall apples from the orchard and anything else he could get his snout into! His main purpose in life was to get fat, little knowing that this was also hastening his own demise. It wasn't unusual for a visitor to be told smugly, 'Wait till you see our pig!'

The neighbour would then be taken out to the shed to inspect the pig. He would duly compliment you on your fine specimen and admire his rotundity saying, 'You must be giving him the best of feeding. He's coming on great.'

We loved to get on the pig's back for a ride around the yard but the crafty creature would scrape along beside the wall and force us off. We wondered if he felt the cold in winter, because apart from a few short hairs he looked rather pink and naked! The fatter the pig got, the nearer his day of reckoning came. When my father announced that Will Casey was coming the following morning, we all feared the worst. I ran out to watch the poor condemned animal, for the last time, as he ambled contentedly around the yard, oblivious of his impending fate. I knew that another pig would replace him in a short time and that life on the farm would continue as usual.

Next day, my father and mother rose early. We were dispatched to the river for several buckets of water, which were put to boil in the big black pot over the fire. Our hearts weren't in it. Then the creamery cart was brought into the cow-house and the pig was tied down on his back, to the sides, with strong ropes. The poor animal was making an awful commotion. He seemed to sense that things weren't looking good. Many a pig led his owner a merry dance before being caught on the day of execution.

This was the moment for me to disappear to the 'Gorry Beg', which was the field on our farm furthest from the house. Even at this distance, I could hear the agonised, dying roar of the pig as Will Casey stuck the knife into his heart. His life-blood fell into a strategically placed enamel bowl. This would later be made into black puddings. When I returned, the poor dead pig was tied to a ladder in the cow-house, where the carcase would drip overnight. The smell was overpowering.

Next day the animal was shaved, having been doused liberally with scalding water. Will quartered the sides and set them to cure in salt-petre, a preservative, in a big wooden barrel. After some time, it could be hung on hooks in the ceiling where the smoke from the fire would make it brown and hard. Farmers were very proud of their flitches of bacon dangling from the ceiling! It showed that they were good providers. My brother salvaged the bladder to blow up into a football.

My mother made the puddings with a little help from us. Our job was to take the pig guts to the river and let the water run through them until they were as clean as a whistle. We had to turn them inside out several times. These would provide the casing for the puddings. Back in the kitchen my mother had her sleeves rolled up and was busily stirring the blood in a big bowl, mixing in allspice, pepper and salt, herbs, onions and barley. Every farmer's wife had her own secret ingredient.

The casing was attached to the narrow end of a bottle. The broad end had the glass knocked out by heating it all around with a candle and then neatly tapping it off. My mother kept filling it up with the mixture and forcing it through the narrow end and into the casing. She ended up with long strings of pudding, which she pricked all over to prevent them from bursting, before placing them in a pot of boiling water and allowing them to cook over the fire. They were later cut to size and tied with string.

We were sent to neighbour's houses with pork steak and were always assured of a great welcome and maybe a sixpence.

'Was it Will Casey ye got?' one neighbour asked. 'He always does a good clean job.'

We couldn't see anything good or clean about the whole business. In the absence of refrigerators, you could only hold so much fresh meat yourself, so this might explain people's sudden bursts of generosity! Puddings were also distributed and the neighbours gave us some back when they killed their own pig. My mother was very particular about which neighbour's puddings she would eat. Hygiene didn't feature very largely in some houses at the time and one can only imagine the conditions under which some puddings were made!

Heartless children that we were, we chose to conveniently forget our friend the pig, as we tucked into fresh pork steak, or black puddings, bursting their sides in the frying pan, and tasty pig liver. Anything other than salted bacon was a novelty. Unfortunately, the pork steak only lasted a few days but the puddings were put to season on the crane near the fire and survived a bit longer.

Before very long, we were back to our old bacon and cabbage and thanks to our pig, we were well-fed and happy for another year. We even got fond of the new pig, though we knew that a similar fate awaited him!

GOOD WHOLESOME FOOD

We knew exactly where our food came from: we had thinned turnips, picked potatoes, collected the eggs from the hen-house and seen Judy the cow being milked. An occasional pot of Chiver's jam was as processed as our food got!

When I was growing up, food wasn't varied, like it is today. What we did have though, without realising it, was healthy, organic produce, free from pesticides, artificial manures and additives.

I can still see my mother, her blue cross-over apron smudged with flour. She had her sleeves pulled up to the elbows, bent over the big, round basin on the table, mixing dough. She sang 'The Black Velvet Band' as she mixed the flour, bread soda, salt and sour milk together so I felt that she must be happy. I wasn't too happy though, because I had to give the fire fifty blows to make it light up to bake the cake. I had a quick, sad flashback to the fate of the poor chickens as I turned the wheel. When the dough was worked to her satisfaction, she kneaded and flattened it out with her knuckles, making a cross in the middle. She then transferred it to the hot bastable, or baking pot, which was also lightly floured, and covered it. She took a shovelful of 'spreece' from the heart of the fire and put it on the lid to ensure the cake got cooked on top. After an hour, provided the fire was kept going, she took out a lovely cake of bread which she put cooling on the outside windowsill.

As well as the more ordinary, everyday, cakes, mother also made caraway seed bread – which I hated – and currant or sultana cakes, which were great. We'd often pick at the currants while it was cooling! Of course, our favourite was apple cake. This was mostly made in the autumn, when the apples were plentiful, and we were called on to help peel and slice them. By placing rows of apples, wrapped in newspaper, on shelves in the dairy, they often held until Christmas. The flour for the bread came in big white bags and had to be kept dry, and safe from mice and mites. Some people washed the bags and used them as sheets when the flour was used up. Sugar came in big bags also. People bought a lot of provisions in bulk.

The dinner, in most country houses, consisted of 'bacon and cabbage', the meat coming from the poor sacrificial pig! Cabbage was grown in every garden each spring and was the popular accompaniment to bacon. However, supplies would have run out by December or January so there was a long wait for cabbage and other greens.

But the main event, on any self-respecting dinner table, was the humble spud. I can't imagine what my father would think of a dinner without potatoes! And there were lots of them. Big, floury, laughing ones, straight from the earth, begging to be eaten. With a knob of homemade butter sliding over the top and a mug of buttermilk, it was a dinner fit for a king!

Indeed, many children of that generation were reared almost exclusively on 'goody', which was bread soaked in milk and 'pandy', a delicious combination of mashed potatoes and butter. Sometimes, raw onions were added to make it even more mouth-watering Though setting the potatoes, cabbage and turnips was labour intensive, and I can remember thinning and weeding with less than nostalgia, gathering in the harvest of vegetables made it all worth while. We were set now for the winter.

We had a separator in the dairy for dividing the milk from the cream. It was a complicated piece of machinery to assemble, with lots of pans and shiny steel parts, all of which had to be thoroughly washed after use. There was a handle at the side, which set it all in motion. We loved to see the rich stream of cream coming slowly out the pipe at the back, and sneaked a finger underneath for a lick. The cream was then put aside for making butter in the churn This was one more way to be self-sufficient.

Churning the butter was a daily chore. We had a little glass container, which was used for small amounts, but out in the dairy stood a big, brown wooden churn, lying on its side on a kind of frame, for the serious butter-making. When you heard a plopping sound, this was the signal that the butter was made. It was washed several times in the coldest water available to extract the milk and my mother worked repeatedly on it with paddles to squeeze out the last drops. It was then salted, divided and a pattern traced along the top. My mother sometimes sold it in the nearby town where it was well received. The shops didn't accept everybody's homemade butter. There was an old custom that anybody who visited while the churning was in progress should take a turn. If a neighbour had bad wishes for you, he might put a curse on the cream and stop it turning into butter! Drinking, arguing or singing was not allowed during churning either!

My mother made apple jelly in the autumn by boiling apples, and straining them through a muslin bag hung over the back of a chair, out in the dairy. You couldn't squeeze the bulging bag, even though it was very tempting! It had to drip slowly over the space of a few days and then the clear, pink juice was boiled with sugar and put into pots. How delighted I was to receive such a delicacy when I was a boarder in school.

Our parents always had fowl so if you wanted a menu change from bacon and cabbage, my mother thought nothing of going out in the yard and twisting the neck of a chicken or a duck. Alternatively, she might also chop his head off with the hatchet! He was then plucked and drawn and boiled in a big pot over the fire. Mam added plenty of onions, carrots and dumplings and it certainly was tasty! At Christmas, of course, there was roast goose with all the trimmings.

Plucking the goose was an operation in itself. My mother would tie an old scarf around her head and sit on a chair in the middle of the kitchen. In front of her she placed a box to hold the feathers, which would later be used to fill pillows. The tearing, ripping sound went on until she had plucked her clean, saving the two wings for brushing around the fire. There were feathers everywhere, in hair and eyes and up our noses! Mother then singed the pinfeathers over the fire and hung the bird in the dairy where it dripped bloodily for the next few days, the liver and gizzard having been put aside.

The year the American relations came to stay, my mother had reared a couple of dozen chickens in anticipation, so that she'd have a tasty dinner on hand at the drop of a hat! On one never-to-be-forgotten occasion, my parents were gone overnight, when our visitors returned unexpectedly and my teenaged sister, Eileen, who had hardly ever even watched my mother prepare a fowl, had to do the whole chicken thing herself! I seem to remember that the tongs were used to remove the entrails! She will never forget it, but she knew the Yanks had to be fed at all costs.

Eggs were usually in plentiful supply. My oldest sister favoured duck eggs. On Easter Sunday we competed to see who'd eat the most, but I never managed more than three. My father maintained that the rising sun danced on Easter morning but we were never up early enough to confirm or deny this old myth My brother was a great hand at making scrambled eggs and he also used eggs for making 'exotic' dishes, like meringues, when our parents were gone to town! His burnt offerings were nothing like the Pavlova we are used to eating today!

We took bread and butter sandwiches to school, with a bottle of milk, for our lunch. How I envied one girl, who sometimes had a big yellow orange. In the autumn, we had lots of plums, pears and apples and we also went picking blackberries from the hedges. Sometimes we sold bucketfuls to our local shopkeeper, Mick Duggan, for a few shillings.

Then there was visitor food. This was always the same and consisted of ham, tomatoes and sweet cake. We'd run up to the parlour the minute the visitors were gone out the gate, hoping to find leftovers. All you'd get would be the fat from around the outside of the ham and a few miserable sweet crumbs!

We used river water for making tea, cooking and washing, and it was fresh and pure after its journey from the Galty mountains over rocks and stones. It had its own distinctive, brackish, taste and never having known any other, it was the definitive taste of water for us. We never got sick. The only illness I remember having that necessitated calling a doctor, was when I had the whooping cough. Anything else was treated with a dose of castor oil, which tasted horrible. 'You'd be eating it all day,' a man once said to me. I think he meant that it had a habit of repeating!

Bit by bit, we noticed the changes. First, it was the shop bread and creamery butter. Then there were sausages and tinned peas, and corn flakes instead of porridge. Oxtail soup, in a packet, was another wonder. Biscuits and Gateaux cakes found their way into most cupboards before too long and many women stopped baking. Mossie, one of our card-players pretended to have trouble with the french word and called it a Gatyaxe cake!

If you found a cake of bread, like my mother used to make, nowadays, it would be in an organic food shop and would cost a fortune! People have actually lost their taste for pure, natural food. Our taste buds have become dulled over the years and we need strong spicy sauces to bring the food alive. Perhaps it's because we have so many new cultures joining us, plus the fact that we have more money in our pockets to experiment, that people's daily bread could now vary from foccacia, naan to pitta !

THE MARKET BUS

I remember waiting at the top road with Eileen when I was about eleven for the bus that would take us to the circus in Cahir. The drive in the bus was almost as exciting as the circus!

Travelling on a bus when I was a child was 'a big deal'. My father often went to County Council meetings in Clonmel and Thurles by bus and once he went as far as Sligo. But I had only ever got a ride in the pony and trap.

When I was eight or nine years old, however, this was to change. My mother decided to take me with her on the bus to Athy, Co. Kildare to visit my father's cousin. I was so excited! I decided to take my doll with me to share this great adventure, so I set about the task of making her a suitcase. After all what self-respecting doll could go on holidays without luggage! To create this masterpiece I got an old shoebox and threaded mother's sewing needle to attach a cloth carrying handle to the side. I can't remember how it turned out, but that didn't matter in light of the tragedy that followed! I lost the needle! This was a mortal sin in our house We were warned over and over to be terribly careful with needles because if they got stuck in you they could make straight for your heart and kill you! My whole holiday was overshadowed by the great worry that I could die any minute. I daren't confide in my mother.

The other thing that stands out about that first bus trip was that Mam gave me a bar of fruit-and-nut chocolate for the journey. This was a great novelty in itself! I scoffed the whole lot immediately and felt terrible. Of course, the bus had to keep going, so I had no choice but to throw up into my red pixie cap! I could never look a fruit-and-nut chocolate bar in the eye again. And I can tell you that I was more careful with sewing needles, too!

In the early fifties a 'market bus' came on-stream to take local people to Mitchelstown every Thursday, which was market-day. It was often a fair day as well. This bus would start from Burncourt and travel the 'top' road, picking up passengers as it went. It would stop anywhere; outside houses, shops, boreens or gateways. A lot of people got on in the village of Kilbehenny. It was a new lease of life for many who had no other motorised transport to town.

Our bus conductor, Steve, was a small, fat, bespectacled man and he was from Cork. He knew everybody's name and business and was a friendly, patient soul and a great favourite.

Molly, a fine block of a country woman dressed in layers of overlapping dark clothes, big strong black boots and a coloured headscarf stuck out her hand to stop the bus. She carried a cloth meal bag, which aroused a bit of curiosity among the other passengers.

As Steve did his rounds, collecting the fare, which was around two shillings, he chatted amiably to his customers. Each new passenger was scrutinised from top to toe as they boarded the bus. The ladies admired each others costumes (suits) and coats. The men were in their top coats and peaked caps and sat bunched together in the long back seat, one or two enjoying a smoke. There was a lively hum of conversation as the bus trundled along, stopping every couple of miles while the passengers pushed in to make room for the latest newcomer, as it became ever more crowded. The women discussed the price of eggs, the crops and the local scandals. The men's chat centred on whether 'Tipp' would beat Cork in the up-coming hurling final and would they get a fine spell for the hay.

There was plenty of time for husbands to have a drink in the pub while the women bought the groceries in the Co-op, a fresh loaf of bread, a pound of sausages, or a pig's head. There was also a trip to the butchers for a bit of stewing beef for tomorrow's dinner. They'd have a look at the wool in Doran's knitting shop and maybe chance a pair of those new nylon stockings. When all the shopping was done, they trooped wearily back to the bus, sinking back in their seats. Steve was stretched out in the front seat having a smoke. The women furtively eyed each other's baskets and bags. That soft brown parcel of Mrs. Flynn's was definitely from the drapers. Had she bought a new skirt or blouse! Where was she going?

But there were other purchases as well. Women brought bundles of cabbage plants, day-old chicks, ducks and geese on to the bus. Molly arrived with a 'sucky calf' in a bag, his head sticking out! (We now knew the purpose of the bag) Steve, not batting an eyelid, settled them both up front near the driver. There was new energy to the conversation now. Snippets of gossip about whom they'd seen going in or coming out of the Co-op were exchanged. There was outrage at the price of commodities. Mrs. McGrath patted her bulging bags of messages with a sigh of contentment. You couldn't beat a nice bit of pig's head.

The calf made a half-hearted bid for freedom, but Molly's size nine boot kept him firmly under control.

Steve always helped the older people off and would carry the heavy bags across the road to their gates and see them safely into their houses. When Molly's turn came, he noticed that her brother was waiting, with fresh straw lining the horse drawn cart, all prepared for the new arrival. Between them they manhandled the calf off the bus and on to the cart while the rest of the passengers craned their necks unashamedly to watch the drama.

'Did you get a good look, Steve, was it a bull or a heifer calf?' asked Johnny curiously.

'You're asking the wrong man,' laughed our conductor. 'Sure I'm a city boy, born and bred!'

I might be coming home from school around market bus time and the old lady who lived down my boreen would be getting off, Steve helpfully lifting down her bag.

As we walked home together, she'd say, 'I know why that old Steve is all *plamás*, helping with my bag and all. He's very glad of my fare every week!'

She was certain that Steve kept all the fares for himself.

Being a nice little girl(!), I sometimes carried her big bag of messages but as we neared her house she would slyly dismiss me with a wave of her hand, saying, 'Run away now. Don't be expecting anything and you won't be disappointed.' It was a salutary lesson.

Everybody was in a good mood on the bus after their day out. Some of the men, fortified by bottles of stout, were anxious to give their happy feelings expression.

'Give us a bar of 'Tipperary So Far Away', Johnny!' someone shouted, and song followed song as the bus made the homeward journey, flanked by the majestic Galty mountains on one side and the Knockmealdowns on the other.

My mother had been travelling by car to town for over ten years, but when my father died all that changed. Since she had never learned to drive, she started using the market bus too. She walked across two fields to meet the boreen that led up to the top road, so it was quite an expedition and could take all day. But there was no rush.

However, as time went by, the number of car-owners increased and the market bus wasn't as popular. When the one man buses came into operation, our dear Steve was made redundant and the drivers now collected the fares. Naturally, they hadn't as much time or opportunity to talk to the passengers, so the whole market bus journey experience changed.

There is still a bus going from Burncourt to Mitchelstown on a Thursday, but you have to get to it before it starts its journey, which isn't always convenient for some. Buses don't stop along the way anymore so that lovely personal service provided back in the fifties and sixties by Steve and his market bus is sadly one more thing relegated to history.

THE MAGIC OF WIRELESS

It sat on the kitchen window with a white cloth draped reverently over it. Because we couldn't understand how it worked we were mightily in awe of this ingenious device that brought the world into our kitchen. Life would never be the same again!

Oh, how clearly I can remember the excitement and thrill of our first wireless! It was the early fifties and we had listened to Micheál Ó'Héhir's commentaries on the hurling matches in other people's houses. But to have a wireless all of our own was surely a dream come true.

I didn't know, or care then, that the wireless was the brainchild of a famous Italian called Guglielmo Marconi, who patented his invention in spite of his critics, in 1896. Britain transmitted its first spoken broadcast in 1919 and the B.B.C. was launched in 1922. The rest is, as they say, history. The wireless may seem pretty ordinary to young people of today, used to so much technology, but for us it was a dramatic break-through. My mother once remarked that you couldn't properly appreciate the wireless unless you had your own. You were rather at its mercy in another's house but at home you could be the boss of it. My father decided that the best part was the knob for turning it off!

It was a local schoolteacher – an ardent wireless buff – who introduced the radio to our house.

'Wait 'til you hear what we're getting at home,' I boasted to Patricia Connolly at school, 'a wireless, and we'll be able to get all the pop songs.'

The rather bulky apparatus, including wet and dry batteries filled the small front window of our kitchen, and blocked out most of the light. It was a small price to pay. Our technician friend made mysterious connections to receivers at the back, plus aerial joinings from the big pole in the front yard. Finally, we touched base with Radio Eireann all the way from Athlone. What a great moment it was when a strange man's voice spoke to us in our own kitchen. We were informed, entertained and enthralled and stayed up until the transmission ended and the man wished us good night. My father said good night back to him as if they were already old friends.

The wet battery was a clumsy contraption with a handle on top, which had to be carted off regularly to the garage for re-charging. Then, the acid bubbled merrily away for another couple of weeks, depending on how much it was used.

A few bars of 'O'Donnell Abu' heralded the start of transmission each evening. If you wanted daytime programmes, there was the B.B.C., which brought us our first soap, 'Mrs. Dale's Diary'. We found it hard to understand their accents. Radio Luxembourg, however, was a firm favourite, It wasn't long before we knew all the words of the Top Twenty hits. The ones that come to mind were 'She Wears Red Feathers', 'The Story of my Life', 'Be my Life's Companion'. 'Love Letters in the Sand' and Ruby Murray's 'Softly, Softly'. Watching me gyrating around the kitchen, dreamy-eyed, as Pat Boone gave his romantic rendition of 'Remember You're Mine', my mother worried about inflamed passions and undermined morals.

'Would ye have your prayers off as quick, I wonder,' she snapped, as she observed us once more with our ears glued to the wireless as we tried to memorise the words.

She was wasting her time worrying about us, because we were hooked, as surely as the youngsters of the twenty-first century are hooked on their music idols. Our parents enjoyed listening to Din Joe's 'Take the Floor', Paddy Crosbie's 'The School Around the Corner', 'The Ballad Maker's Saturday Night' or 'Take Your Pick'. This was hosted by dynamic presenter, Michael Miles, on Radio Luxembourg and provided heart-stopping moments, when the competitors wondered would they open the box or not! My father would try to have all his jobs done outside and a nice fire going, so he could sit down to enjoy this show. It ran from 1953 to 1960 and was extremely popular, as was Hughie Greene's cash quiz 'Double Your Money'. The high point of this was the £32 question. He also compered the legendary 'Opportunity Knocks' programme, which very often was the first rung on the ladder for young hopefuls.

Many sunny Sunday afternoons were spent listening to Micheál Ó'Héhir's compelling commentaries of the hurling and football matches from Croke Park. Now that we had our own wireless, we felt that Micheál was one of ourselves, as he sucked us into the excitement, passion and frenzy of the cheering crowd in the packed stadium. We were inclined to even blame him a little when Tipperary lost the game!

We experimented with the short wave band, where we located foreign stations and mysterious wavelengths. Hilversum, Berlin, Bergen. As we moved the tuning dial back and forth we picked up strange, guttural accents accompanied by crackling static sounds, which we suspected might be coming from outer space! My brother was more interested in locating some Scottish station, where he could savour Jimmy Shand and Jimmy Cameron's Ceilidhe Bands. That was the closest you could get to Irish traditional music at the time, which was rarely played on Radio Eireann.

An old lady who lived next door decided, after much deliberation, to install a wireless. She soon became an addict, developing an unnatural obsession with the weather forecast. One evening, on my way home from school, she asked me, 'What did the man in your wireless say about the weather for to-morrow?' She seemed to think that each house had its own individual forecaster and presenter!

Later on, when transmission hours were increased, we had the sponsored programmes to enjoy. Donnelly's sausages, presented by Niall Boden, immediately springs to mind as my own personal favourite, because of their catchy jingle which went:

> *Yes, it's true they're the talk of the nation,*
> *A sausage excitingly new,*
> *So new that it's caused a sensation,*

And Donnelly's make them for you.
With two wrappers for double protection,
The best that your money can buy,
The last word in sausage perfection,
They are skinless and easy to fry.
So the next time you visit your grocer,
Tell him no other sausage will do,
To his other suggestions say, 'No, sir',
It's Donnelly's sausages for you.

I have no idea who the writer of this little verse is, I wonder if he/she is still alive.

No one doubted Leo Maguire's sincerity as he signed off from the Walton's programme each week with a plea from the heart: 'And Walton's last word is, if you feel like singing, do sing an Irish song'. The famous Irish Hospitals' Sweepstake programme usually rounded off the night with Ian Priestley Mitchell urging his listeners to buy a sweepstake ticket. His dulcet tones almost lulled us to sleep with the happy possibility of winning a fortune.

Makes no difference where you are,
You can wish upon a star.

Glen Abbey, Gateaux and Mitchelstown Creameries sponsored programmes and all put their own individual stamp on the week. We eagerly followed the fortunes of 'The Kennedys of Castleross' for many years, too, but eventually the format changed and new programmes came on the air. Jimmy O'Dea, Harry O'Donovan and Maureen Potter were hugely popular at this time and gave much pleasure and entertainment to their listeners. Across the water, the B.B.C. provided music for every mood from Victor Sylvester to Winifred Atwell's dazzling piano performances of the current hits to the lively rhythms of cockney dance band leader Billy Cotton.

There were programmes that we hated, like 'The Cattle Market Report', 'The Stock Exchange News', the sea area forecast and the performances of the Radio Eireann Light Orchestra! I can remember that my father was as excited as a child when Santa Claus made his Christmas broadcast – reading out children's letters and warning them to go to bed early on the big night. Small wonder that I still believed in Santa at the age of fourteen!

The wireless was definitely the first outside intrusion into our homes, changing us in subtle little ways. The pop songs fuelled our teenage fantasies and set us apart, somehow, from our parents' generation. The daily news bulletins connected us to all corners of the country and further afield, so we weren't so dependant on neighbours for our information. Even the weather forecast was a big help to the farmer in planning work for the week ahead. However, card playing, which was a regular fixture in our house, continued uninterrupted in spite of the wireless. There was a clash, sometimes, on Sunday nights when we wanted to listen to the 'Top Twenty' from Luxembourg and they wanted quietness to keep track of the count,

'Will ye turn down that blooming thing, we can't hear our ears,' my mother would shout and 'will you look at the time, ye should be gone to bed hours ago.'

Television exploded into our homes in the sixties, capturing our imaginations with its immediacy, excitement and mystery and the wireless was relegated to second place. It is still going strong, though with many more stations nowadays to give a bigger choice. Long ago, we only had Radio Eireann and in retrospect, I think it offered a very comprehensive and varied programme menu with a personal style of delivery. Unlimited choice can be confusing and ultimately is no choice at all.

I'm glad that Marconi ignored the sceptics of his day and pursued his dream. We certainly owe him an awful lot.

UNFORGETTABLE AUNT ESTHER

Aunt Esther was fascinating because she was half American and so different to anybody we'd ever seen before. She didn't comply with any rules! She changed everything and I was devastated when she left.

Aunt Esther was my uncle's widow – my father's sister-in-law – and she hailed from Mayo. However, she had spent long enough in America to qualify as a Yank. I was about ten years old when I heard that she was coming on a visit. We were thrilled to be entertaining our very own Yank visitor at last!

My mother had to bring the house up to visitor standard so there was feverish whitewashing and wallpapering for a few weeks. Our room was allocated to Aunt Esther so we were going to be temporarily re-housed in the dairy, which we loved. My father even cleaned the kitchen chimney, so it felt like Christmas When she finally burst into our thatched farmhouse, she turned our lives completely upside-down. She brought us clothes, 'candy' and comics. She kissed us. Often! This didn't go down too well with my painfully shy, teenaged brother, who avoided her like the plague. She told us we were pretty. Actually 'cute' was the word she used, which we weren't too sure about. Aunt Esther surpassed all our wildest expectations with her long red nails, her accent, her hair and her lipstick Not to mention her outrageousness!

One night at the rosary – a holy and sacred ritual in our house – she rose from her knees half way through the trimmings and declared, 'Hey guys, how about we finish this to-morrow night? We must have prayed for half the folk in the parish.'

WELL, what a thing to say! I was shocked to the core and waited for the sky to fall. Stranger still, my mother hid a smile and cut the rosary short. I heard her telling my father later that they probably had no religion in America and that we must make allowances. Aunt Esther changed the whole atmosphere in our house. My parents were happier and more carefree as they laughed over something funny she'd said or done. This reflected well on us of course. My mother had the task of making sure that she had a comfortable bed and plenty to eat. Our guest considered bacon and cabbage a real treat and she was 'tickled pink' to see it bubbling away over the kitchen fire in the big black pot.

Visitors came to see our Yank and there was a general party feeling around. My father played the accordion in the middle of the day. Chores were neglected and only essential farm-work, like going to the creamery, got done. We excitedly gave Aunt Esther the guided tour around the farmyard. She picked her steps delicately through the dirty henhouse in her fine shoes. She examined the big brown hen hatching in the wooden box and I told her that the chickens would be out in a week.

'Why are the eggs marked with a cross, honey?' she enquired.

'Oh, that's so they'll all have chickens in them and there will be no glugars,' I answered knowledgeably.

'Oh right . . .' said Aunt Esther, a little puzzled.

'Who's that son of a gun with the long neck?'

'Run quick or he'll eat you. That's the ould gander and he's pure wicked!' I warned her.

The calves, with their drooling mouths, poked their black and white heads through the half door of the barn and tried to suck her fingers. She was having a ball. The grunting pig, fattening in the shed caught her attention.

'Why is he so round and fat – surely he needs a bit of exercise?' she ventured.

'Oh no, we want him that way, the fatter the better, so we'll have plenty of bacon and pork when we kill him. And lovely puddings too,' I added.

'Oh no honey! That's so cruel! How can you even think of killing him? Oh, the poor creature!'

We took her to Mass in the horse and trap, which she thought 'wonderful' and I was delighted with the attention she attracted. My mother was a bit put out that she wore nothing on her head. When asked about this she laughed.

'That's old-fashioned, Hannie. In the States nobody cares.'

A neighbour, who had known my uncle, shook her hand and asked, 'Are you staying around long?'

'Oh my vacation is for three weeks. I got to see all the folks and view the sights.'

'Well, begor then, there aren't too many sights hereabouts,' said the neighbour, scratching his head, 'unless you go down in the Caves over there beside ye.'

Mitchelstown Caves
(Photo courtesy of Kathleen English)

'I'd be too scared to go down in that big, dark hole. What about my good clothes? I prefer the sunshine and a look at the pretty Galty mountains right behind the old thatched house.'

Because we lived next door to these famous Mitchelstown Caves, we had the opportunity as children to visit often. In those pre-electricity days oil lamps and candles were used to negotiate the underground descent, which greatly added to the mystery and magic. We later became aware, of course, of the Caves' huge archaeological importance with speleologists, cavers and visitors from all parts of the world coming to examine and admire their spectacular drip stone formations, caverns, glistening calcite curtains, stalagmites and stalactites. It has become an ever increasingly popular tourist destination in recent years, and is now superbly lit throughout to highlight the ancient, timeless treasures in all their glory. Aunt Esther didn't know what she was missing!

We showed her a short cut across the river to Molly's. She was the lady who kept a terribly untidy house and asked a lot of questions. We were treated to tea and mouldy biscuits.

'Don't you ever feel like dressing up and going to town, Molly?' Aunt Esther asked, looking around in bewilderment at the chaos and mess of the kitchen.

'Sure, what good would that be to me?' replied Molly, who lived alone. 'Who would I tell my story to when I came back?'

It rained the day Aunt Esther left. My tears matched the weather. The house seemed very dull and empty without her as we returned to our ordinary, every day routine. The smell of her perfume lingered briefly in the room when we reclaimed it. I wrote to her straight away on a page of my school copybook. I was sad and annoyed at her for taking away the magic. The letter wasn't posted. Maybe I hadn't the price of the airmail stamp! Sadly, Aunt Esther never received the childish scrawl, begging her to come back. Even if she had, I doubt that the atmosphere she created that first time could ever be duplicated.

I still have that letter though, packed away with other memories from the past. When I read it I relive again that summer long ago, when Aunt Esther changed our family for a few unforgettable weeks.

LIGHTS IN THE FIELD

Lights in the field could have supernatural implications. Or they could be
connected to exciting real live strangers and a boy called Drew.

Nowadays, if you step outside your house on a winter's night, you
can't see the dark anymore. Between street lamps from nearby
villages, lights outside farms and places of business and security bulbs
in front of houses, the countryside is no longer completely dark.

In my early childhood, before the advent of electricity, in winter the
dark was inky black, apart from the occasional moon and scattering of
stars. No wonder it was such a fertile breeding ground for boody men
and ghosts. Occasionally, my parents would spot mysterious lights
in the fields at night, which were put down to Jackie the Lantern
or spirits of some kind. We would all go out to have a look. They
weren't in the least bit bothered and rather welcomed the diversion!
It would cause a little shiver of fear in us children though! Being
realistic, the most likely cause was poachers, after salmon in the river,
or young boys lamping rabbits. One way or another, it didn't matter.
My mother maintained that lights were 'lucky'!

We often had neighbours dropping in for card games in the winter
and it would be late when they started for home. One particular night,
our neighbour, Hugh, spent hours walking around our big field, because
he couldn't find the way out until dawn broke. The old people said that
if you turned your coat inside out that you would get your bearings.
Hugh would have been glad of Jackie the Lantern that night! Another
old lady, who visited regularly on Sunday evenings, saw ghosts and
apparitions, at our gate. The dark caused people to imagine all sorts.

One time though, when I was twelve or thirteen years old, we had
real, warm welcoming, lights in our field. It was an evening in late

autumn, when my mother answered a knock on the door. She found a strange man standing on the doorstep, smiling apologetically.

'Sorry for bothering you, Mam! My name is Tom McDonald, from, er . . . from Scotland. I was wondering if you would let us park our caravan in your wee field by the stream for a night or two? There's my wife and myself and our boy and another couple, friends of ours, the Campbells. We're touring your beautiful country.'

'Come in out of the cold,' said my mother matter-of-factly, only half understanding his unusual accent, 'and we'll have a chat about it. That should be no bother at all.'

'Johnny,' she called to my father, 'we have a visitor.'

My father, dressed in his old clothes, was bringing in sticks and bushes for the fire. After putting them down in the corner; he shook off the dust and extending a hand, warmly welcomed the stranger.

'You'll have a cup of tea,' said my mother, hanging the black kettle over the fire.

I hung back, watching and listening. And wondering if the son would be around my age!

'Will ye be staying around long? my father asked as he settled a big stick at the back of the fire. 'Maybe yourself and the Missus and the others would come up tomorrow night and we'll have a bit of a dance. I can make a bit of noise on that old melodeon.' He smiled modestly, pointing to the box on the shelf up beside the Sacred Heart picture. My father used any excuse for a hooley.

'Ach, sure we'd be only delighted,' said Tom smiling broadly. 'We'd love to learn about your Irish culture. The others will be thrilled. What luck to happen on a musical family! Are you sure it's O.K to stay in the field? We won't be any trouble and we won't frighten the cattle. They'll probably be curious when they see our lights. We have gas lamps, you know. By the way, we love the sound of the wee stream.' he went on, as he drank the cup of strong tea my mother had prepared.

Wee stream indeed! We considered that to be a big river! Hadn't we fished in it and used the washtub as a boat, as we sailed off with the current one time. We couldn't wait to meet the rest of the gang but had to wait until the next day. In the meantime, our friend, Hugh, made his nightly visit and his first comment was, 'Ye have great lights in the field with the campers.'

We were probably the talk of the parish, because campers and caravans were few and far between at the time. Anyway, my parents got ready for the night. A few of the neighbours were notified and my mother made a currant cake and an apple tart. My father cut several big blocks of wood and we said the rosary early. Normally we would include visitors in the rosary, but we had a feeling that the campers weren't rosary type people.

Around eight o'clock, the neighbours gathered in and then our Scottish friends arrived. They brought a tin box of biscuits. The boy, Drew, was nine or ten years old and quite shy so I never got chatting with him. The adults, on the other hand, weren't a bit shy, and danced Highland Flings with abandon, the ladies holding up their skirts shamelessly as they twirled around. We were enthralled. My father played tune after tune and we danced half sets. Tom McDonald asked my mother to dance an old time waltz and she coyly hesitated. She joked that she didn't sing or dance since she got married! I sang a song, 'If I were a Blackbird', and my sister did a recitation. My father gave a fine rendition of his favourite 'Old Skibbereen'. It was a happy night. We ate mother's cake and drank cups of tea from her best china. Later, my father asked them what part of Scotland they hailed from.

'Penicuik, near Edinburgh,' volunteered Tom. 'If you're ever in Scotland, be sure and call.'

'Ah sure, it's very unlikely, but you'd never know,' said my father, taking a long drag from his Woodbine.

'What would you like to do when you grow up?' Mrs Campbell asked me conversationally. I was delighted with the attention. Nobody had ever been interested in my future before.

'An air hostess,' I replied, with a sudden burst of inspiration.

'Ach sure, you're pretty enough for the job anyway,' said her husband.

'Don't be putting notions like that into her head,' intercepted my mother sharply. 'Next thing, she'll believe you.'

The party ended and our visitors departed into the night. We were sad to see our campers leave us a couple of days later. The only sign of their presence was a flattened patch of grass where the caravan wheels had been. On the following days, I'd snatch a glance in the mirror in the kitchen as I passed. My mother caught me though and wasn't long about shattering any illusions I might have been harbouring!

'Have you nothing better to do than to be admiring yourself in the glass? Don't think you're good-looking now, just because those Scottish people said it. People like them are all *plamás*. It would be more in your line to bring in a *gabhail* of sticks. The fire is nearly gone out.'

The final chapter was written regarding our Scottish friends, when several years later, my sister and I found ourselves in Edinburgh. As our money started to run out, we decided to look up Penicuik. We were welcomed with open arms and stayed a few nights with the McDonalds and they recalled the wonderful holiday they had in Ireland. They said that night of music was the highlight of their trip. They marvelled at how spontaneously my parents had dropped everything to show hospitality to complete strangers. But weren't we only delighted with the diversion? We loved any excuse for a party. And the lights in the field near the river brightened up the dark, (and our lives) even if it was for only a few nights!

THE TRIMMINGS OF THE ROSARY

The only thing that relieved the tedium of the rosary was when a neighbour or stranger was roped in and we waited to see what kind of a twist they'd put on their decade!

When I was growing up, the nightly recitation of the rosary was as inevitable as the setting of the sun. It was simply unthinkable, to go to bed without first going on your knees. What awful retribution might lie in store for the hapless heathen, who closed his eyes with such an omission on his conscience! After supper was the time. The oil lamp, on the back wall of the kitchen, was lit. The cows were milked and the hens and ducks locked in for the night. We were almost stowed . . .

'Thou O Lord wilt open my lips.'

We all rushed to our knees at the long bench, rosary beads in hand, as my father said his opening lines. It was better not to be the one who had to resort to counting her Hail Marys on her fingers and risk going over the ten. My mother's chair swayed backwards and forwards as she got into the praying mode and she doled out the decades between us. My father sat in his favourite chair by the fire. Since the accident to his leg in the forties, he wasn't expected to kneel. The rest of us were in varying positions of reverence (or irreverence!) and rose to the challenge when our decade came up. I thought it very unfair that, being the youngest of four, the decades had run out before it came to my turn, so I only had 'a go' if somebody was missing. We looked for ways to make the time pass quicker, like trying to make each other laugh, which wasn't too difficult, or following the journey of a black beetle crossing the cement floor. If Trixie, the terrier, was around he might bare his teeth at the beetle, and cause a bit of a titter. My mother would banish us to the porch if we got too unruly, where we sobered up very fast.

Our trimmings took as long as the Rosary itself. They included prayers for Cardinal Mynzenty who was in prison, a prayer for fine weather if we had hay cut, one for mother's 'special intentions', the litany of the Blessed Virgin, the Pioneer prayer, the Memorare and prayers for the souls of dead relations, friends and neighbours. I had a map of the rosary in my head and knew when we were on the home stretch. Then we said some more silent prayers of our own, so it was with a great sigh of relief that we finally rose from our knees.

Anybody who happened to call when we were 'at' the rosary quietly went on their knees and automatically joined in. They weren't properly welcomed until it was finished. These could be card players, who came twice a week, and the rosary would be said earlier on those nights. We loved when outsiders joined us. We waited to see what kind of an air they'd have to the Hail Mary! One old lady visited almost every Sunday night and she'd have us in fits with the queer lonesome way she said her decade. The rosary didn't work any miracles on our piety at all I'm afraid.

We would often say our decade as Gaeilge and everybody, including my father, would answer in Irish. When we progressed to secondary school and thought we knew it all, we tried to confound our parents with our bit of Latin chanting 'ora pro nobis' in mock piety during the response to the litany. Our parents bore it all stoically. They knew that it was a fad that would pass! As we grew older and our interests widened, it became harder and harder to get us together to pray. My father, the opportunist, would remark if there were a few of us sitting around the fire, 'Why don't we kneel down now for the rosary while we have the help?'

When we started going to dances, my mother would round us up beforehand, or if that was impossible, it was taken for granted that we would say the rosary on the way to the dance! This was a source of much amusement to our less pious friends, who wanted to know if we were thinking of joining the nuns!

There's a story told of a young Irish priest who was sent to the African Missions and introduced the rosary to his newly converted flock. They were all praying very earnestly in the church one evening when he was called away urgently. He selected one of his trusted senior parishioners to take over until he got back. He was gone rather longer than he expected and imagine his surprise, on his way home, to see the church still lit up. Curiously, he tiptoed inside, just in time to hear the elder member announcing jubilantly to the congregation, 'The 147th sorrowful mystery, Judas stabs Pilate in the back'!

The mission stalls outside the church did a roaring trade in rosary beads. They could hardly keep up with the demands from all the rejuvenated Catholics who had been frightened out of their wits by missioners' sermons. All you had to do then was get them blessed in confession and you were away on a hack. A beads bought in Knock was highly valued and a Lourdes one even more so. Some were highly ornate with gold crosses, maybe even containing a saint's relic, while others were carved out in expensive mother-of pearl. The most treasured beads of all were those got in Rome and blessed by the Holy Father himself. Sure prayers on the like of those beads couldn't fail to get answered!

I remember going to a *Fleadh Ceóil* in Swinford in the sixties and I left my green rosary beads under the pillow in the guesthouse. I wrote to the owner asking them to post it on to me as soon as possible. Doesn't it typify a lost age of innocence when prayers and devotion meant so much?

There could never be a right time now for a family to pray together, unless you could squeeze it in between the commercials during 'Coronation Street'. Young people, nowadays, might not be in the same room as their parents, not to mind praying with them. But we were old hands at saying the rosary, knowing at a young age, what mysteries to say each night and reaming off long trimming prayers that we didn't understand.

Maybe it wasn't such a bad way to end the day!

VISITORS

Visitors invariably changed the atmosphere in our house in a positive way. Here was a chance to either bask in unaccustomed attention or else become invisible to pursue nefarious acts of one's own, in the safe knowledge that parents were much too engrossed to register our absence!

Having visitors to our thatched home was great. First of all, it transformed our parents. Their affability and joviality towards the visitor somehow rubbed off on us. All our misdemeanours were temporarily forgotten, as we presented a united front to our guests.

We had card players on a regular basis and even though we weren't allowed to play when we were small, a congenial atmosphere was generated. But card players weren't like people who came especially to see you. We loved real visitors. We preferred my mother's friends, because women were more likely to bring sweets and pay you attention! Sometimes, on our return from school, we'd be thrilled and excited to spot a bicycle propped up against the wall.

'Is it a man's or a woman's bike?' I'd shout.

Women's conversation was far more interesting, not to mention mysterious and enlightening! And we might also get a 'go' on the bike when nobody was watching. Or sample the ham and sweet cake that might be left over from the tea! Having said that, there were two gentlemen cousins of my father's, whom we always welcomed warmly because they never failed to slip us a half-crown. We hung around shamelessly in case they forgot!

We had a neighbour who visited us regularly and joined with us in the recitation of the rosary As well as enjoying her recitation of the decade, she would later provide even further interest. When it came to the supper, she would try to discreetly slip her ill-fitting dentures (which were only worn for 'appearance') into her bag. We'd

Having a dance in the yard

be anticipating the moment of course and would always catch her!

Then there were the VIP visitors. These were entertained in the parlour. We would have helped my mother prepare for such an occasion, dusting and sweeping the seldom used room and bringing in turf and sticks for the fire. The best tea set would be taken out of the cupboard and arranged carefully on the parlour table. Our mother wouldn't let us near the good cups and always washed them and put them away herself. That was fine by us! On one never-to-be-forgotten occasion, she was preparing tea for the local government official who was canvassing in our area for the up-coming election. She dropped most of the precious tea set with the excitement and it smashed to smithereens. To her eternal shame, the great man had to drink his tea out of a common kitchen cup!

If our relations arrived unexpectedly, in motorcars, my sister Eileen was immediately dispatched on her bicycle to get ham, tomatoes and a Swiss roll. The more thoughtful ones brought their own provisions. We loved 'visitor food' and watching from the sidelines, willing them not to polish it all off! My father might be out working in the fields but he was promptly called in to join the company. He was a very sociable man and loved to entertain, often producing the accordion and forgetting all about the work outside.

The visitors we really liked were those who stayed the night, though perhaps my mother wasn't quite so enthusiastic, as it fell to her to find extra bed space and blankets. When our cousins from Kildare came to stay, we created mayhem. It was a great novelty to have children of our own age staying the night. We weren't going to waste one minute of it and hardly slept at all. Cousin Peggy was very welcome, too, and we exchanged stories, rhymes and jokes, often till the small hours.

An aunt and uncle from Boston, came in the late fifties. By then we had a car and we saw Killarney for the first time. I think it must have been in America that Aunt Ciss heard of Killarney. Uncle Ned loved our old grey mare, Dolly, and suggested that he take her back to the States with him instead of my aunt if she didn't stop nagging! We organised a farewell party for them and Jimmy Fitzgerald from Mitchelstown provided the music.

We loved to see Jack coming, footsore and weary from travelling the roads of Munster. His mongrel dog, Spot, was a sad looking specimen, but Jack loved and respected him anyway. He insisted that, 'There are papers going with that dog.'

Here was a man who entered wholeheartedly into the rosary, though we tittered shamelessly at the variations he brought to his decade as well. Afterwards, he entertained us with his favourites 'The Grand Old Lady Murphy O' and 'The Rose of Mooncoin' in return for a makeshift bed in front of the fire. His version of the song differed a little from the conventional one. There was a part that went:

> *When the thrush and the robin their sweet notes entwine*
> *On the banks of the Suir that flows down by Mooncoin.*

Jack had his own interpretation:

> *Where the thrush ate the robin and the big ball of twine*
> *On the banks of the Suir that flows down by Mooncoin!*

Jack was a travelling man with an honest, saintly nature. He wouldn't harm a fly, so nobody refused him a bed for the night. We are indebted to him for his simplicity, integrity and good humour, and the atmosphere and flavour that he brought with him. I remember hearing that he died on the same day as De Valera so we lost two good men together!

When a visitor would get up to leave, my mother might say, 'Wait 'till I put you past the gander,' as she walked out to the gate with them. Ganders were notoriously wicked and kept in houses instead of watch-dogs in times past.

Visiting is not as popular nowadays with all the other distractions around. It's by appointment only or you'd find nobody at home. But isn't there something exciting about the sound of the dog barking or a knock on the door? It could be anybody!

THE THRESHING

The arrival of the big, red threshing mill created a carnival-like atmosphere. The distinctive booming sound as the machine rose and fell could be heard for miles while the high spirited meitheal, with shirts open to the waist, chatted and joked as they piked the sheaves aloft. They knew that there would be a great night's dancing later . . .

As children, undoubtedly, the day of the threshing was the high point on the farm calendar for us. The man responsible for all this excitement was our neighbour, Dan. He owned the big, red, lumbering contraption that lurched and heaved into our haggard every year, bringing such joy to our hearts. On reflection, I'm quite sure the poor man found his work rather tedious and repetitive. The culmination of my father's work of producing a yearly crop of wheat was the threshing of the grain. We would be thrilled to hear our parents talking, for a few days before, about the upcoming event and relaying the news to the neighbours. We had to fit into Dan's schedule. Many farmers would be looking for him in the month of September.

Our kind, West Cork master, let us off early from school for this important occasion, on condition that we would ask permission *as gaeilge*. As we ran home, we could hear, in the distance, the rise and fall of the threshing mill. Our father explained to us that a thick belt connected the machine to the pulley wheel of the tractor and this created a different sound when it was threshing and when it was running free.

I dropped my school bag in a heap on the kitchen table and ran out to the haggard at the back of the house, where it was all happening. This was a very streamlined operation. I watched a neighbour on top of the big stack of corn, piking the sheaves to a man on the threshing mill, who then cut the twine and fed them into the belly of the whirling machine.

I ran around to the opening on the side of the machine, letting the yellow grain flow in a golden, mesmeric stream through my fingers into the waiting bag. This post was always manned by Dad, who ensured that there was no spillage and that the bags were replaced as necessary. Two other men were making a rick out of the threshed straw, which came from a larger opening in the threshing mill. This would be used for animal bedding in the cow-house and other sheds later on. The job continued all evening, the big machine quivering and throbbing relentlessly, powered by the old Massey Ferguson tractor. Dan sat contentedly on the seat puffing his pipe.

When the work was completed, Mother had a big meal of bacon and cabbage ready for Dan and the helpers. Some got porter as well, and they slugged it back thirstily, pulling bits of straw out of their hair. They were well pleased with their day's work.

'By god Johnny, you were lucky to get the fine bit of a day,' said John from Skeheen.

'I'd say that's as good a bit of whate as ever I saw,' commented another neighbour, raising a bottle to his head.

We were lonesome as we saw the tractor pulling the big old threshing mill slowly out of the yard. It barely fitted through the gate. My father carefully collected up all the cords and twine and put them away for safe-keeping. Then the bags of grain were heaped together, ready for the lorry, which came from Mitchelstown. When we saw the truck disappearing down the field, we knew that the threshing was really over for another year. Later the wheat would be graded and a cheque sent to my father.

Inside, things were hotting up. After everybody had been fed and the cups and plates put away, the table was pushed back against the wall. The chairs and the long bench were arranged along in a line. The late September evening was drawing in but the big wood fire cast a warm glow on the company. We stole out to the dairy where the empty lemonade bottles were stored. We discovered that if you put the dregs of each bottle together you got a sizeable amount of sweet fizzy drink! Then we raced into the kitchen to watch the dancing. Local, single women with pale faces and red lips had been drafted in specially to match the steps of the erstwhile pike wielders. They didn't need much persuasion to dance! They knocked sparks off the old cement floor with their strong boots as they swung around shouting, 'Mind the dresser!'

There was much playful banter and innuendo. Many a match was made at these threshing dances.

My father never tired of playing the accordion and Sieges of Ennis, half-sets and waltzes followed in quick succession. There was more tea later on and the bottles of stout were disappearing by the new time. A few old men sat over the fire telling ghost stories. The hair stood on our heads with fear. We thanked the lord that our names didn't start with Mac or Ó because they were linked with the banshee and foretold a death with a lonesome keening, blood-curdling sound. We heard about the *cóiste bodhar* – a sinister, black, death coach with headless horses and a headless coachman, which passed in the night through the boreens and fields of Ireland, picking out its victim . . . Mother forgot to tell us go to bed and we stuck it out to the very end, though our eyes were heavy with sleep and our heads reeling with images of the ghoulish tales we'd just heard!

Finally, the *meitheal* headed for home, the men with their pitchforks slung over their shoulders. We would return the favour when their threshing day came. My parents sat over the dying embers of the fire, recounting the day's events.

'Did you see that Jamsie slugging back the porter? I hope he doesn't fall in the ditch going home.'

'Never mind about him,' said my mother. 'Do you think we'll get a good price for the wheat?'

'I'd say we'll do fine.' 'Twas a grand day . . . and night,' said my father contentedly, as he lit up his last cigarette of the day.

FOOTNOTE: *Meitheal* is an Irish word meaning a group of neighbours working together on a job.

WASHDAY

Wet clothes draped over chairs. Steam on the windows and on my mother's glasses. Glistening cement kitchen floor, with the big bathtub taking centre stage. Mother's nerves frazzled as she tries to organize her troop of reluctant helpers.

My mother mostly picked Saturdays for washing the clothes, when she'd have help. We were dispatched to the river for numerous buckets of water. My brother was older and bigger and had to bring a bucket in each hand. We spilled half the contents, laughing, slipping and chasing each other round the field on the way back. Children can extract fun from any situation. My mother would scold crossly.

'If ye would stop the skibbing and tinkering, ye might bring up a full bucket. Go out now, let ye, and get some sticks for the fire. We need lots of hot water if I'm to get this washing done.'

Being the youngest, I was given an easy job.

'Give the fire fifty blows,' ordered my mother.

The fire machine was a marvellous invention. When you turned the big wheel it blew air along a pipe under the grate and with a bit of luck, got the fire going. I'd blow the machine fifty times and then run quickly out of the kitchen before my mother caught me. I wouldn't bother to look back to see if the fire was lighting or not! Mother rolled her sleeves up above the elbows and got out the big washtub and washboard. Set against the side of the tub, the latter would be used to remove stubborn stains like those on the collars of shirts by rubbing them up and down on its corrugated surface. With a big cake of red Sunlight soap she would create lots of foamy suds as she poured in the pot of boiling water. We were kept busy keeping supplies replenished.

By this time my mother had a damp, rosy complexion. Her hands were red and raw from rubbing the clothes and her blue-patterned, cross-over apron was splotched with water. The cement floor was awash too. She got cracking on the cleanest clothes first and when it came to the dirtier farm clothes and towels, the water slowly turned a dark shade of brown. All the clothes then had to be rinsed in clean, cold water. She would ask us to help her to squeeze them out by holding on to one end, while she turned and twisted the other end of the sheets and shirts. You needed good, strong arms for the job. The clothes would then be draped across the backs of chairs, ready for hanging out.

By now, the distinctive smell of wet clothes permeated the kitchen and the air was hot and steamy My father stuck his head around the door and seeing the disorder and chaos, resignedly asked, 'Will it be a tay dinner to-day?'

My mother hadn't time to answer him as she wiped the steam from her glasses. Bit by bit, the pile of dirty clothes got smaller. Our legs ached from our constant trips to the river, as our mother tiredly finished the job. When we helped her to empty the tub of dirty water, and put all the newly washed clothes into it and transported them to the clothesline in the garden, she seemed relieved. Then they were all pegged and the long pole inserted in the middle to raise the clothesline high in the air. It was rewarding to see the clean washing blowing in the wind.

'I hope to God it doesn't rain, now,' she would say, looking worriedly at the sky.

We went inside and tried to get the kitchen back to normal, while my mother busied herself frying rashers and eggs. My father had a big fire going and the wet floor was beginning to dry up a bit. My mother had taken off her wet overall and took a well-earned rest when the supper was over.

An eye would have to be kept on the weather now and all the clothes whipped in at the first sign of rain. We would all be on the alert. They would then be aired on the backs of chairs turned to the fire. I liked this bit. It was very cosy as you snuggled in the corner, surrounded by sheets and towels, watching the steam rising. You could still smell the fresh air from them! Mother would test a dress or jumper by putting it to her cheek to make sure it wasn't damp before we put it on. Next job would be the ironing of items like shirts or school clothes.

But that was a whole other day's work!

REMEMBERING FARM ANIMALS AND PETS

My parents grieved when an animal died, but as my father dug the burial hole he would comment philosophically, 'May the harm of the year go with her!'

Being the youngest of my family, I relied a lot on animals for company, and what wonderful friends they made. Some might have only lasted for a season, while others became a big part of our lives. We were on nodding acquaintance with the donkey and the pig, having been thrown unceremoniously off their backs many times. The horses and cows were our friends in a more impersonal way, and newborn calves and lambs were interesting and amusing for a while. We once had a pet lamb, called Woolly, who turned into a very bold sheep. She would follow us around, even coming into the kitchen, butting us with her head and causing general havoc and mayhem! She had no interest in being out in the fields with the other sheep. She considered herself a household pet, like Sally the dog!

Dolly the white mare was a fixture in the family for many years. We needed her for transport and along with Nancy, our other horse, they did all the work on the farm. Dolly, however, was on the road a lot taking us to town and to Mass in the trap and needed proper shoes. My father would take her to be shod regularly. I begged to go with him one time to have a look.

Our friend Tom, the blacksmith, a big powerful man with strong, brawny arms, lived about two miles away. His face shone with sweat from the constant overpowering heat and his shirt sleeves were rolled up to show great bulging muscles. The distinctive, acrid smell of horse dung, coal and burnt hoof parings hit you as you approached the forge which was a bustling hive of industry. A few neighbouring men stood around, some with horses to be shod, others there for the diversion. This was a chance to get a heat of the fire and hear the latest scandals.

All eyes were on Tom, the principal player in the drama, as he heated an iron bar in the heart of the huge fire for a time, the sparks scattering like stars. He pushed the hand bellows in and out to redden it. Then he deftly grasped the iron from the fiery furnace with a big black tongs. It was hurriedly placed on the anvil to be twisted, shaped and moulded into a horse shoe while still hot, the hammer strokes echoing around the countryside. I had to stick my fingers in my ears to stop the ringing! After a quick dip in cold water, it was swiftly secured to Dolly's pared hoof. Dad assured me that it did not hurt at all. The shoe was hammered in securely with three nails and the mare was all set for a few more months.

Dolly paid for her keep, but still, it was to the small animals and fowl we gave our hearts. Trixie was a lively, clever little mongrel terrier, and was my companion on all my childhood adventures. She was mostly white but had a brown patch on her ears and over one eye She would disappear for hours to chase rabbits and this was a cause for worry, but she always came back. When she had pups, I lay on the hay, watching them suckle and willing their eyes to open! One day, much to my delight, they stood squarely on their little short legs and surveyed the world. With their ears erect, heads to one side, they made a few endearing, tentative barks.

I suffered with them, when the neighbour came with his knife and cut off their tails, leaving them with little bloody stubs. I enjoyed watching their playful antics as they tumbled and played. I had my own favourite, who would crawl on my lap for a sleep . . .

Then, one day, mother said, 'We'll have to find homes for those pups. One dog is enough for us.'

With a heavy heart, I watched them leave, one by one. At least, they weren't consigned to a watery grave, as so often happened.

The following Christmas, Trixie went missing. I searched high up and low down, walked every field and boreen, whistling and calling her name but to no avail.

'She's chasing rabbits again, she'll come back' said my mother consolingly. But she never did. Even Santa failed to lift my spirits that Christmas.

I 'rescued' a lame chicken once, covering its sore leg with a clean, white bandage. Of course, this turned into a filthy rag in minutes as chickens are not known for sitting down with their 'leg up' for long! I don't think she enjoyed my company at all.

I remember the excitement with which we waited for chicks to hatch out. We would hold the eggs to our ears to hear the first faint chipping sounds. They were cute and cuddly for a short time, until they became plain, gangly and hen-like. Then we lost interest.

Ducks were hard to tame, but goslings were an entirely different matter. Mother entrusted a few weak or delicate goslings to my care over the years. Perhaps, she realised that they would never reach maturity, so they lived their short lives, surrounded by loving attention. Would they have been better off with the goose? Most of my goslings died prematurely.

My sister and I caught a baby rabbit as we returned from school one day. He was hiding behind a clump of rushes and I stole up and covered him with my coat. My father took the trouble to make a hutch and enjoyed the rabbit as much as we did. Because he became so tame, we let him run about freely in the yard and garden. He followed us everywhere and we had great fun together. At night he would stretch out in front of the fire. The cat, however, didn't recognise him as one of the family and had him for dinner. We cried when we found the little white tail.

Our pets certainly enriched our lives and taught us how to care for and respect God's creatures. It also showed us that sometimes, perhaps, animals stand a better chance if left outside with their natural parents!

Dolly lived to be very old. We all mourned her passing and treasured the long and loyal service she'd given us. It was truly the end of an era for us.

TROTTING TO THE FAIR

There was an economic war in Ireland the year my parents got married
– 1932. Cattle prices were so bad that some farmers opted to throw their
calves in the river rather than taking them to the fair. There was a song,
when I was young that went:

> *Trotting to the fair*
> *Me and Moll Maloney*
> *Seated I declare*
> *On a single pony . . .*

Doesn't it sound idyllic? But fair days were far from being all fun
and frolic! However, they did play a very important part in the
farming and social life of Ireland, fifty years ago. This was the forum
for selling animals that had been painstakingly fed and looked after
for two or three years. It represented a major part of farmers' incomes.
Fairs were held in every town in Ireland, three or four times a year.

My brother, John was often wakened around 3 a.m. on a late
spring morning, to go with my father to the fair in the local town.
This was eight miles away, and could take hours, depending on how
contrary the cattle were. They would try to get into every open gap,
field and neighbour's yard. A nosy animal stuck his head in the door
of a woman's kitchen one morning, as she was having her breakfast!

The dress code for farmers going to fairs was always the same. An
old coat that had seen better days, tied in the middle with binder
twine, a peaked cap turned backwards, and a pair of black Wellingtons.
It can't have been easy to walk nine miles in these rubber boots, but
they were the best protection against mucky, wet roads and streets
full of cow dung.

Some farmers took their cattle to town the night before and they
were secured in an area known as 'The Pound' at the top of the town.

It was important to be there early so you could pick a prominent place to display your animals for the jobbers. These were men from every corner of the country who bought and sold cattle all the time and they would do their best to knock you down in price. They wanted to get their business done and get on the train home. They denigrated and insulted your stock declaring them to be 'skin and bone' and only fit for the knacker's yard. They walked around the animals, prodding them with sticks, then turned on their heels, as if totally uninterested. There might be a swift u-turn.

'Will you take twenty-five pounds, it's my final offer and I'm laving myself short at that,' declared the jobber. My father decided to hang on for another while.

But it was cold and nothing was worse than having to drive that lot home again with no money in your pocket. The square and indeed, much of the rest of the town, was choc-a-block with every type of animal from sheep to cattle to horses and donkeys. Some farmers had brought their dogs, as well, to drive the cattle, and these were now sitting, exhausted, on the ground, tongues hanging out. A woman was selling homemade butter and laying pullets. Men had no interest in hens. My father maintained that they all died in debt and were only a nuisance around a farm.

'Come on, John,' my father said. 'We'll go in to Caplices's restaurant for a bite.'

A neighbour agreed to keep an eye on the bullocks for half an hour. There was an appetising smell of boiled meat and onions wafting through the door and they headed for a long table, where several hungry men were already noisily slurping their food and belching loudly with appreciation.

'What will ye have?' asked a rosy cheeked young girl.

It was rough and ready but this was no time to be fussy.

'Give us two plates of Irish stew, if you have it,' said my father.

They had bacon and cabbage every day, so this would be a change. They both wired into the steaming dinners and had tapioca after with a dollop of strawberry jam on top. With renewed energy, they were ready to do business again. Back in the square, a man was knowledgably tapping one of our bullocks with his stick, as if to assess his weight and worth. He backed off as my father approached and moved a little distance away. He was what was known as a 'blocker'. He might want the animal for his friend at a reduced price and would keep the genuine jobbers away. These men were a curse at fairs.

My brother met an old man, a friend of the family and got sixpence, which he promptly spent on bulls' eyes. He was getting fed up of hanging around.

'John, will you see if there's any sign of Mam. She said she'd drive in the pony and trap later to take us home. I hope she won't be going back on her own!'

Some shopkeepers had erected barricades in front of their premises for protection. The streets and walls were destroyed and the pungent smell of animal excrement permeated the town. The business people dreaded fair days, even though it brought extra trade. A fine day would be a great blessing, but picture the scene of misery if it rained. As the day wore on, the town emptied out, as farmers sold their cattle and made for the pubs. There would be lots of rows later and disputes over 'luck pennies'.

Many a man only drank on fair days and it went straight to his head. I heard of one intoxicated farmer who would sit into his cart and creel, slap the pony on the rump and they'd head for home, the man unconscious on the floor of the cart.

One time, my father gave an old, half-dying pony to a friend of his to sell, telling him that he could keep anything he got over five pounds, for himself. My brother, who was attending the Christian Brothers' school in the town at the time, hung about this comical character to watch his antics. He was highly amused to hear him extolling the speed and agility of the pony to a prospective buyer.

'Whatever you do, don't give him oats or you'll never catch him!' The sales pitch got him well over the asking price and my father got what had been arranged!

But there were still cattle to sell. As the evening drew in, Dad was getting tired and worried about his prospects. Then out of nowhere, came the jobber, who'd looked at the cattle earlier.

'Did you not sell them? Ah, sure, out of pity, I'll give you twenty pounds each for them.'

'No', said my father, 'you can keep your money. I'm taking them home again. I'm not giving them away for a song.' He thought that another jobber might come along and offer a better price. It was hard to know what was best to do.

Talking of songs, the ballad singer was doing a roaring trade selling his pages. He had all the words of the popular old 'come all ye's' of the day and performed them with great heart and gusto. He needed no microphone! No doubt, he had been fortified by liberal quantities of stout. A fine crowd of happy revellers gathered around to listen, infected by the festive atmosphere. This was their day out. Back in the square, my father lit up a cigarette and looked at my brother.

'What will we do, John? I see your mother is waiting outside the store. She wants money for messages. Will I toughen it out or what?'

'Give them to the jobber for what he offered,' replied John in a tired voice. He was in a hurry to go home. He was far more interested in books that farming. Just then, the very man approached, swinging his stick, his brown hat cocked to one side.

'O.K. seeing as I'm in a good mood, I'll rob myself and give you ninety-five pounds for the five. What do you say?'

The jobber spat noisily on his outstretched hand.

'Is it a deal or not?' I'm not hanging around much longer. I've a train to catch.'

'I suppose so,' said my father slowly shaking his sweaty hand, 'though I think that you're getting the best of the bargain.'

'Who're you trying to cod?' said the jobber. 'But what about a luck penny, or will we go in for a drink instead?'

'I don't drink,' said my father, 'and John is too young for public houses. Give me my money and let me off.'

'I'll drive them up to the train myself so and spare you the job. I'll put them in with a few more I bought earlier,' said the jobber affably, happy now that he'd made a good bargain. The railway had closed in Mitchelstown towards the end of the forties but it still operated on fair days for several years and was the most popular method of

Fair day (photograph courtesy of John Tuohy*)*

transporting cattle. The jobber peeled off some notes from a huge dirty wad and handed them to my father, and the luck penny was given. The transaction was complete and they went their separate ways. For an instant, John had a pang of regret because he knew all the cattle by name. My father was glad to have sold them and he hadn't got such a bad price in the end.

'John,' said my father, 'here's a 'fairing' handing him a half-crown. 'I couldn't have managed without you.'

My brother ran off, in high glee, to buy his favourite *Hotspur* comic. My mother was pleased, too, and bought all the extra little items for the house that she'd been putting off, like oranges, mothballs, candles, knitting wool, hair ribbons, towels and a new tablecloth for the stations. There was fresh meat for to-morrow's dinner, sausages for the supper and a big bag of sweets for us children to enjoy. My father related the day's happening as the horse trotted home, their big, plentiful bag of messages overflowing in the well of the trap.

'I won't be sorry to get out of these Wellingtons and give my toes a good roasting at the fire,' said my father wearily as he took a long, satisfying, drag of his cigarette. 'Didn't we get a fine dinner in Caplice's though, John?'

But there was no answer. My brother was fast asleep!

A DIFFERENT CHRISTMAS

Turkey, holly, decorations, cards. Families sitting before a roaring fire pulling crackers and eating pudding. High spirits, goodwill to all and cardboard cribs. But what if something is missing . . . ?

Christmas was always magical in our house when I was a child. Santa Claus or Daddy Christmas (my mother's name for him) never failed to find us, no matter how hard the times. How glad I was to know that he never had economic problems, unlike our parents, who had many demands on their money. I often wished that he would bring them something they really needed. But it seemed he was only interested in bringing presents to children. The grown-ups would smile slyly and tell us that they had read in the paper that Santa was sick and couldn't make his rounds this year. We were so worried and desperately prayed for his recovery.

The weeks preceding the great day were exciting. Father would go to the wood for berried holly, where it grew in abundance. We then had the task of painstakingly cutting off the leaves and threading them on to a long piece of string with a packing needle. We often had sore hands after they were all strung together, but it was worth the effort. When the two lengths of holly leaves were hung diagonally across the ceiling, with a coloured balloon tied in the centre where they met, there was an instant festive feeling.

Now, the kitchen looked full of promise. The remaining holly was placed in a bundle on top of the big cupboard, except for a few twigs stuck behind the clock and the Sacred Heart picture, where the berries glowed in the light of the big open fire. As the Christmas cards began to arrive, they provided further interest, lining the walls and standing along the sideboard in colourful rows. Afterwards, we would use them for keeping track of the count in the '110' card game. Sending them out was a chore. My mother would have a small table pulled up to the fire with cards and envelopes at the ready. She selected suitably holy cards for nuns and priests and important people. The ones with robins, snow and Christmas trees went to the less fussy! The fire would have gone out by the time she had finished them all. She would declare every year that she'd stop sending them altogether, but then was disappointed if even one friend failed to remember her!

The crib got pride of place on the back window, the cardboard Joseph and Mary kneeling by the manger where baby Jesus lay. We really lived the Christmas story and felt sorry for the child being born in such a miserable stable. We knew what it was like to be cold on a winter's night. It was a great relief to know that the ox and the ass kept baby Jesus warm with their breath. We faithfully said our one thousand Hail Marys every year on time for Christmas day. I remember notching them up on the inside of the closet door. Mother said that it was a Christmas present for Jesus and a kind of insurance that Santa would come. We had given him our list when we wrote to him at the North Pole, but we felt that God and Santa were somehow in league and we wanted to keep them on our hands!

We tormented our father, telling him to hurry up and clean the chimney or Santa mightn't come. Ours was such a big and wide one we felt sure that, at least, he'd have no bother climbing down. I always borrowed my father's sock for hanging up near the fire on Christmas Eve as it was bigger than my own and I wanted to get as much as possible!.

We were awake at first light on Christmas morning, shivering with cold and excitement. We never caught Santa in the act but we sensed that he was only just gone when we got up. Hadn't my sister seen his lights in the sky one Christmas Eve? Outside, the frost had formed delicate tapestries which decorated the thatch, window ledges and gates and the big field sparkled and shone in the early dawn light. It was a truly perfect Christmas morning.

We raced into the kitchen. Our old, every-day fireplace was glitteringly transformed into a magical toy-shop. Dolls and shiny bugles spilled out of bulging socks. Jig-saws, games and sweets were strewn on the floor. Hair slides, ribbons, books and clothes littered the chairs and. brightly coloured tinsel hung off the black, every-day crane, shimmering and shining. We woke our parents as we shrieked with surprise and delight.

'Oh great, I got fireworks. I wonder how do they work.'

'And I got a doll in a cot, Oh, she's gorgeous!' cried my sister, through chattering teeth.

'Would you just look at what John got,' laughed Kate, 'custard and jelly, the greedy gut. I wonder how did Santa know what a pig he is.'

But there were many, many other exciting and interesting toys and trinkets over the years. We got whistles that would wake the dead with their discordant, penetrating sound, spinning tops, colouring pencils, toy jewellery, gollywogs, tea-sets, bull's eyes and oranges. One unforgettable Christmas, Santa brought me a doll's go-car (buggy). We always got useful articles of clothing like socks, underwear and ribbons, but it was the toys that made Christmas special for us. By the time my mother got up, my brother had the two packets of jelly eaten and I had used up all the fireworks.

'Pity, I'd have loved to have seen them go off,' sighed my mother.

We dressed in our new finery, courtesy of Santa Claus and headed for Mass. The choir sang the ever hauntingly beautiful 'Silent Night'. The neighbours greeted each other warmly with good wishes for the holy season, as they picked their steps on the slippery churchyard.

'Happy Christmas John, 'tis a fine hardy morning.'

''Tis that Jim, but thank God it's dry. A happy Christmas to you.'

The day had lots of treats to come yet. The smell of the goose roasting in the bastable over the fire assailed our nostrils and reminded us of how hungry we were. My mother's potato stuffing was perfect every year. This was a dinner to be savoured, all the more precious because it was a rare event. The rest of the time, it would be back to plainer fare like bacon and cabbage. We didn't much care for the plum pudding that followed. We ate the sweets we got from Santa instead and played excitedly with our new toys. I dressed my new rag doll lovingly and put her to sleep in her shoe-box cot. Our father might suggest a game of Ludo (our favourite board game), or cards, or try out one of the new games we got from Santa.

Christmas was delightfully predictable, year after year. I thought it would never change. Then, one terrible November day, when I was about thirteen years my mother delivered a mortal blow. She took me aside and disclosed the earth shattering news. There was NO SANTA CLAUS!

If she had told me that my father was an axe murderer, I couldn't have been more shocked. No Santa Claus! But where had all the lovely gifts come from over the years? Why had my brother and sisters kept up the pretence? My friend in school had been right after all. It was my mother putting the toys there! I wondered where on earth she'd got the money to buy them. Years later she told me that she would start saving the pennies from September onwards, so that Santa would be able to pay his annual visit!

So now it was Christmas again, but one with no Santa! We still had the holly and decorations and the cards strung in rows against the back wall of the kitchen. One of my sisters had holidays from boarding school and the other was home from training college. My brother was on a few days' break as well. It should have been perfect. But something was missing . . . On Christmas morning, I got up at a respectable hour. No more early scrambling out of bed, rushing to the kitchen to see what Santa had left. No more excited shouts of, 'What did Santa bring you?'

Father lit the fire in his usual leisurely fashion, a little bundle of straw first, then kindling and a big block for the back to throw out the heat. He always had his first cigarette of the day at this time, much to my mother's disapproval! Mother cooked rashers and sausages in the frying pan, which she placed on a brand over the fire. The goose was on the table, waiting to be stuffed. But it all suddenly seemed to have lost its appeal.

There were four Christmas-wrapped presents with my name on them. The first was a book – *Martin Chuzzlewit* by Charles Dickens from my mother. I tore the paper off the second parcel – another book, *Robinson Crusoe*. The next was a box of chocolates from Eileen. And then, oh no, not another book. *A Tale of Two Cities* from my brother! I cried with disappointment. The last package was soft, so it looked promising. My sister Kathleen had painstakingly knit me a red woolly stocking cap. Anything was better than another book! I was devastated and it probably showed on my face. I enjoyed reading but really, three books! And the writing was so tiny and uninviting looking. It was all too much to bear! If I'd been asked, I probably wouldn't have known what presents I wanted. You see, Santa always managed, somehow, to get it exactly right.

I wore the hat/scarf to mass and hoped people, at least, realised it was new. All in all, my heart was broken. I suddenly realised that Christmas would never be the same again. I was about to enter a new phase! I bet my mother never imagined she'd end up having to tell me the truth. Most intelligent children cop on to Santa when they're about eight or nine! Had my childhood been just a little too sheltered?

SEEING THE LIGHT

What a thrill to flick a switch and watch the bulb come to life. Would the house burn down with all those wires running along under the thatch? The men digging the holes for the ESB created a bit of excitement among the country girls!

I have fond memories, from my early childhood, of sitting by a warm fire on a winter's night, enveloped in the soft glow of the old paraffin lamp. This was attached to the back wall of the kitchen, near enough to the fire to afford light if you were reading, knitting, playing cards or Ludo. My father often pointed scallops with his penknife, which were used to repair the thatch on our roof. You could get your eye knocked out by a piece of flying wood if you weren't careful!

We used a candle to light us to bed in the loft and it cast long flickering shadows around the room. It was a wonder that we didn't set fire to the house! Our fertile imaginations were fuelled with thoughts of monsters, ghouls and ghosts, which came under the general heading of 'the boody man.' The thing was, you were never sure of what might be lurking in the corner. We then progressed to a tilly lamp, which swung from a crook in the middle of the kitchen and showed great light for playing cards. It worked with a mantle – a flimsy, fragile piece of material, which broke easily, and paraffin oil. It was pumped up for extra brightness and emitted an audible hiss. My mother maintained that it was 'hard on the eyes' and never liked it. I think it coincided with her having goitre problems when her eyes were particularly sensitive. Boody men and tilly lamps were soon to become things of the past however. The rural electrification scheme, which happened for us in the early fifties, changed everything.

Many people considered that the ESB poles, which were erected throughout the rural areas of Ireland, were somewhat of a blot on the landscape. However, they were a vital part of the electrification process. Big holes had to be dug to accommodate these poles. On a neighbour's field, the holes were dug and then the weather became so bad that the work couldn't progress. Naturally, they filled up with water as the weeks went by and became a breeding ground for small creatures. One night, as Kate and her husband were saying the rosary, what she described as 'an army of lizards' slid in under the kitchen door. She got a terrible fright! The rosary was quickly abandoned as they swept out the tiny reptiles.

When I heard my parents discussing the hiring of two Ballyporeen men to wire the house, I wondered what it could mean. On my return home from school, one evening, shortly afterwards, all was about to be revealed. I found two strange men hard at work on their mysterious business and I avidly watched their progress. Great lengths of cable snaked up walls and across ceilings. The, as yet, redundant light bulbs, dangled expectantly from ceilings. Light switches were fixed to the wall inside the door of each room and a fixture, called a fuse box, sat importantly on a specially made bracket, attached to the back wall of the kitchen.

The two men were treated almost with reverence. They were about to harness this secret power to light up our home. They were supplied with hearty dinners of bacon and cabbage. My mother dispensed the stout judiciously. She didn't want their judgment clouded in any way! My father listened respectfully as they outlined the great dangers of frayed wires and faulty sockets which unqualified people should never attempt to fix. In spite of all the good advice, it never stopped him risking life and limb when he took occasional stabs at minor repairs. Nothing prepared us though for that great moment when our electrician friend flicked a switch on the kitchen wall and the dangling bulb exploded with light. It was so clear and bright that it was like turning night into day. It lit up every corner of our kitchen, penetrating every little recess, banishing spiders and boody men in one fell swoop!

'Good gracious!' exclaimed my mother, in dismay. 'You can see every speck of dirt. And will you look at all the cobwebs around the clock! . I'll have to do a spring clean to-morrow.'

I ran around the house like a mad thing, to experience, at first hand, the thrill of creating a room full of light just by the flick of a switch. I turned it on and off, on and off!

'Don't be doing that,' scolded my mother. 'You might do some damage!'

Now, reading, homework and craftwork could be done in comfort. We could even read in bed, if we wanted to, though this was frowned upon at first. Country people, who were used to being self-sufficient, were a little bit nervous of an E.S.B. bill coming through their door on a regular basis, so electricity was used sparingly. Two plug sockets were installed in the kitchen and none was considered necessary in the rooms. One socket provided power for the new electric radio, which came later. This relieved us of the arduous task of getting the wet battery constantly recharged. The other socket remained idle for a while until we bought our next item – an electric iron.

My mother thought about a toaster. She said it would be terribly handy the morning of the stations to make toast for the priest, because that was surely the time the bread would fall in on top of the ashes. Since we only had the stations every three years though, it didn't make very sound economic sense. Of course, we never considered making toast for ourselves! Cookers, washing machines or kettles never entered our minds. Getting the electricity, for us, was all about the light. We never imagined its great and far reaching possibilities.

These days, when we have a power failure, everything grinds to a halt. We have become utterly dependent on this marvellous force of nature, which lay unharnessed a few short years ago. Still, when we want to create a special atmosphere, we revert to dining by candlelight. Perhaps, unconsciously, we are trying to recapture the magic of the old days, when days were longer and friendships more enduring.

Or is it that the candle is more forgiving on our wrinkles?

BIG SISTERS

God made us sisters: hearts made us friends.

Aren't big sisters great? Always expected to be responsible and trustworthy. First in the firing line when there's trouble. I could escape the worst of my mother's anger. It had usually dissipated by the time it trickled down to me!

Kathleen was born with a caul. This membrane, which covers an infant's head, was considered a very lucky omen. It was much prized by sea-faring men and was said to ward off all kinds of calamities and evils. She was called after her paternal grandmother and was a confident, capable child. From a young age, she could tackle the horse to the trap on her own, knowing where the winkers, the bellyband, the collar and haimes and britchin went. She often accompanied my father to the fields when he was sowing the oats. He mostly brought her for company. He also took Kathleen (and John) with him to the wood to cut timber.

In the workshop, Kathleen quickly recognised the different tools and would hand them to my father. He might be fixing the horse's tackling, or our shoes, or the handle of the shovel. She knew the difference between the awl, the hammer and the screwdriver.

'Isn't it the dickens, the way she knows all the tools in the workshop?' he'd declare to my mother, as they sat at the fire thrashing out events of the day. She was so useful that she soon became a bit of a pet with him! She attended the nuns' school in Ballyporeen for a year (before entering secondary school in Cahir). We had a white terrier called Teddy at the time, which was very attached to Kathleen. He would wait at the road gate each evening to greet her coming back from school. One winter's day Kathleen was in bed with the 'flu, but nobody told Teddy. He waited for hours in vain.

She took lessons on the fiddle from Dad for a while, but we weren't too keen on listening to her practising! The three of us had lots of fun together; skipping, running races, picking whorts, playing ball, splashing in the river in the summer or visiting relatives and neighbours.

Then our lives began to diverge and Kathleen was disappearing fast on me. She was learning lots of new stuff in school and I became her sounding board. My 11-year-old brain was bombarded with facts and figures! I heard about John Bunyan's *Pilgrim's Progress*, Dantes *Inferno*, and Milton's *Paradise Lost*. She chanted Latin verbs at me, and recited poems in her elocution voice. She rattled off geometry theorems. She quoted

Kathleen's Confirmation

Shakespeare. It was all double Dutch! I worried about how I would cope with such gibberish when I moved on to secondary school. Teaching was the career she picked. In fact, the nuns picked it for her! She had a choice of options, and would have preferred to go to university. But that's another story. Anyway, she taught in Dublin and met her city born husband, Ciarán, there and raised five children. Coincidentally, he was also born with a caul. So weren't they doubly blessed?

It was Eileen who chose the orange over me when I was born! Not that I held that against her! She was called after her maternal grandmother. Next in age to me, she was a lively, imaginative, sociable child and we played together a lot. I remember taking cans of water from a tank at the back to a sand-pile near the house and Eileen would empty them as quickly as I carried them. I was too young and innocent to work out why they were disappearing! Eileen was our messenger! When unexpected visitors arrived at the house she was hastily dispatched on her bicycle to the village for provisions. She was small for her age and considered a bit delicate. Hadn't she a trimming of the rosary all to herself? My mother would look at her and comment worriedly, 'Eil, you're very pale'.

Eileen's Confirmation

Kathleen sometimes wished that she could be pale too, rather than being so blooming healthy looking!

My father bought a tricycle in Dublin when he went to the Fianna Fáil *Árd-Fheis*. This was especially for Eileen, to make her legs strong! She rode it to school and was the envy of all the other pupils. We were bad at looking after it though, and it went rusty from being left outside at night under the rain!

We had a horse called Tom and one hen always laid her egg in the manger of his stable. Eileen would demand Tom's egg for her breakfast and mother would smile as she boiled it in the saucepan over the fire. She was sent on holidays to Araglin, a hilly area about seven miles from home. My parents believed the superior mountain air would bring colour to her cheeks.

We all had summer chores, saving hay and thinning turnips. Eileen and I had the job of raking the last of the hay and taking it into the hay-barn in the ass and cart. We had a play-acting game. It was triggered spontaneously when Eileen began, 'Please ma'am, I'm the new maid!'

There were no props or costumes needed and we could start up anywhere. It might be going to school, thinning turnips or in bed at night. It had a familiar, friendly, comforting feel to it. I was the obnoxious mistress of the house, interviewing the latest member of staff. I would berate and insult her for all I was worth. A Mrs. Bucket type! We carried on with it for years and always assumed the same roles. We also had a 'Hello Missus' routine, which didn't include Kathleen, but she was mentioned as being 'the rich sister'!

The three of us slept in the loft together and devised little schemes and plans. We abbreviated 'last into bed must quench the candle' to LITBMQTC. We allocated names and lives to the mice rustling in the thatch. We smuggled in kittens, read comics by the light of a flash-lamp under the blankets, giggled and made a lot of noise, causing

Mother to sometimes roar up, 'Stop that skibbing and tinkering up there and go to sleep.'

We suddenly became conscious of our appearance, but we couldn't tell if we were pretty or plain. We only got to see bits of ourselves when we made jumps up at my father's shaving mirror in the kitchen! We'd get an all-over look in the shop windows in town, but you couldn't be loitering. People might think you were vain. And that was a sin! Then it happened! Both of my sisters were sailing off on the river of life and I was left sitting on the bank. It would be a while before I put a tentative toe in the water. But I listened and learned. Eileen grew up into a lovely, healthy girl and flew through school. My father looked appraisingly at her one night after the rosary and declared, 'Begor Eil, I think we can forget that trimming now about making you big and strong.'

She got the career that she always wanted – teaching. She was nearly going to be a nun if she didn't get a call to training! She heard that nuns got in the back door! She settled down with a big man, Austie, from near Dundrum, Co. Tipperary, where she still lives and has three grown children.

We went to a lot of dances the summer I was eighteen. I had just got my first driving licence. We became experts at manipulating my father into giving us the car. It involved saying the rosary and making an apple tart. Kathleen and Eileen bought the petrol and I did the driving! One of them loaned me a red skirt and white blouse and I wore it to all the dances that unforgettable summer.

Sisters are invaluable as we go through life. We shared the good times and the bad. We exchanged the maternity dresses and the magical three-day diets. We discussed cures for colicky babies, sulky teenagers, and backache. We went to the sales and bought ridiculously high-heeled shoes we knew we'd never wear, because of our bunions! We still toss ideas around. Like how to live to be a hundred. And look good! Or how to stop our children from putting us into nursing homes!

Best of all, we share great memories. When John, our brother, joins us, we always end up talking about places, events and people that coloured our childhood. Everything from that period seems crystal clear. I wish we could say the same about things that happened last week!

HOLIDAYS

Picture two excited girls waiting at the Rock of Cashel, scouring the road for the car that would take them to Tom and Bridget's house to start the big adventure.

Holidays, for us, usually meant being free from school. We'd rush home shouting, 'Mam, we got the holidays!'

My mother would smile and say, 'Where are they? Did you not take them home with you?'

We went to Carrigeen – my mother's home place – for a week one time and loved every minute with Uncle Patsy, his wife Bridie and their three children Eileen, John and Donal. I remember shelling peas for the first time. We frisked and frolicked with our cousins in the bracing mountain air, eating our fill from the whort-laden heathery bushes. My sister, Eileen had already been on short breaks before this to friends of Dad's in Araglin, where she got on so well that she didn't want to come home! But then we got to spread our wings a little further afield. My father had cousins at the other side of Cashel, two lovely men who called regularly to our house. One summer, when I was about twelve-years-old, they wrote a letter inviting us to their houses. We were over the moon when we were told that we could go. Cashel sounded very exotic and far away. We couldn't wait! However, there was a proviso. Dad said that all turnips and mangolds would have to be thinned and the hay saved before we went.

You never before saw anybody so enthusiastic about getting farm work done. We were on our knees every night praying for fine weather for the hay. We were begging Dad to hurry up and get started. Finally, everything was in order and we were ready to go. We packed our new, brown suitcases excitedly. Should I bring two dresses or three?

Visiting Carigeen in the 1940s – back row from right: my mother, Aunt Nora, Kathleen; front row from right: Eileen and Ann

Eileen wondered would she need a cardigan. Mother told us not to forget clean underwear and to say our prayers every night. My father drove us to Cashel and we met our cousin at the Rock. He was a tall, genial man of about 50 who shook our hands warmly. We had good reason to remember him, because he always stood to us when he came visiting.

'You'll be going to my brother Tom's house first,' cousin William said as we drove out of Cashel, 'and then you can spend the last few days with us. Sure, maybe you can even help out in the shop,' he threw in as an afterthought.

The shop! I'd forgotten about that! I'd never been behind the counter of a shop in my whole life. Imagine being the boss of a shop! Wasn't that what I wanted to do when I left school? In the meantime, we travelled on to Tom's house, past green meadows full of galloping horses. The cows made us think of home but we weren't lonely. We were on a big adventure.

A black and white sheepdog wagged his tail as Tom's wife, Bridget, came out to the car. She welcomed us with a big smile and showed us into her cosy kitchen. She examined our faces with great interest and decided that I took after my mother. Eileen, she noted, was more like my father's side, the side to which they were related. Would they prefer Eileen? They were farmers, like ourselves, so we felt right at home. She put the kettle on straight away and started buttering currant cake. William then took his leave of us, saying he'd see us in a week.

'I'll show ye where the bedroom is now girls,' she called after we'd eaten our fill. 'And don't be in any hurry getting up in the morning. When we have the cows milked, I'll call you to the breakfast. Make yourselves at home now'.

It was nothing short of a miracle for me to find myself in somebody else's house, getting the visitor treatment. No chores to do and no breakfast to get ready. She wouldn't even let us wash up. We explored every inch of the room. There was a jug with water and a matching bowl in which to wash, on a washstand. I hung my dresses in the wardrobe. We put our rosary beads on the little locker near the bed. We wondered if Bridget and Tom said the rosary at night. There were a few books on a table in the corner. We could read all night if we liked. The family next door had heard of our arrival and when we got up next day, there were several pairs of curious eyes staring at us. The youngest was only three-years-old. I thought of all the fun we could have with a real baby for our cabby-house!

Bridget couldn't have been nicer to us. She took us to see the neighbours across the fields. She laughed when we sang the pop songs from the radio. One I can still remember – 'Be my life's companion and you'll never grow old!'

She'd make us sing it over and over for her husband Tom.

We walked to the nearby village with her and helped take home the groceries. We made friends with her dog, Judy, who hunted the cows in each evening. One day Eileen found a nest of eggs in the ditch and Bridget was delighted and made a cake for supper. She had put the eggs in a bowl of water first to make sure none of them floated, which would show that they were rotten.

One night, a friend of Bridget's was holding a party for someone back from America and we were all invited. She ironed my best dress and gave Eileen a loan of a lovely cardigan. I wrote to my mother telling her that I was at a dance and that I wouldn't be home for ages! I remember doing an old time waltz with a man, three times my size and age, and the crowd, sitting around the side, were chuckling and shouting, 'Mind the child!'

Then it was time to go to stay at Willie's house. His wife, daughter and two sons went out of their way to be friendly and showed us around. The family were about ten years our senior so they were quite indulgent towards us. We had a lovely room upstairs. I couldn't get over the fact that they had two stairs, one in the kitchen and another in the front hallway. We had no stairs at home! Only the ladder going up to the loft. Later, when I went to inspect the shop, my eyes were drawn like magnets to the rows of biscuit boxes arranged along the front of the counter. Whole boxes of Kimberley, Mikado and Coconut Creams! There were also big jars of assorted hard sweets sitting out of reach, high up on the shelf. The shop was a pub as well, so we had plenty of noisy male company. One night the men were getting merry and wanted a bit of diversion. They promised that if I sang a song they'd buy me a bottle of lemonade. They didn't have to ask twice!

Eileen read every book and magazine she could get her hands on and there was nobody there to censor the content. We went for walks along unfamiliar roads and marvelled at the novelty of not knowing the people we met! I lost my job as counter hand when I gave out wrong change to a customer! I knew more than ever what I wanted to do when I grew up. We went to the cinema one night, which was a great novelty. I couldn't follow the film at all, but the atmosphere, the dark and the lady selling ice-cream was enough excitement for me.

In the meantime, I was writing home to my mother, begging her to let us stay longer and passing on all the news. I still have those childish letters full of excitement and delight. But all good things come to an end and it was reluctantly that we took our leave of Bridget, Tom, Willie and his wife. We told mother our news a hundred times over. I said that Bridget asked me once if my father and mother went '*cuairdíócht*' at night. Not being sure of the meaning of the Irish word and thinking that it sounded a bit like 'courting' I thought it was safer not to take any chances, so I hastily assured Bridget that they never did. My mother turned away to hide a smile so I knew that this was a good story!

I've been on many holidays but that first time away from home gave me a taste for the road! I will never forget the kindness of Tom, Bridget William and their families towards two children they barely knew. May they all enjoy their place in Heaven.

THE SON AND HEIR

When a son was born to a farming couple, there was great rejoicing even though they might only have a few acres to pass on, but the name had to continue at all costs. Girls were meant to be housekeepers. A friend of mine was over the moon after having her first baby. A neighbouring man asked her what she had and hearing it was a girl remarked, 'Wisha, what harm'!

If my mother never did anything else worthwhile (which I'm not suggesting is true!) she fulfilled her mission on earth when she gave birth to her precious first-born John. Now, she had given her husband a son and heir and the future of the Kearney farm was secured. At least for another generation! John was an intelligent, inquisitive child and very quickly learned who his neighbours were and the names of all the local town lands and villages. He loved books and as he grew older had a voracious appetite for facts and information. His teacher, Dan Casey from West Cork, understood him and inspired in him a love of Ireland, her history, culture and language.

We all had our chores to do on the farm, including John. One of his was to draw water from the river, as he was big and strong and could manage two buckets at a time. Later, when Kathleen went with him, he'd take his own two buckets part of the way and then go back for hers! However, it wasn't all good. Sometimes, at night, he'd sneak up to the back of the house and get the water from a tank my father had built to catch the rainwater. We'd be spying on him of course, and would run to tell my mother! You never got away with anything in our house. He often bemoaned the fact that he only had 'old girls' to play with, and what use were they when it came to hurling and football. My mother would feel sorry for him and compensate with custard and jelly.

John's first Communion

John detested saving hay or thinning turnips and mangolds during the summer holidays. Often he would take a book out to the field and hide it in the drills while we laboured away, weeding and thinning, stung with thistles and nettles and getting clay stuck under our nails. Eileen and I would run ahead up the drill and weed a few patches here and there. Then later on, we'd come upon them and it would help to motivate us to continue with the dreary task. Meantime, John would entertain us with stories of Wolfe Tone or Padraigh Pearse. But we'd have preferred if he'd helped to shorten the drills with us!

As time went by, it became obvious to my parents that he wasn't cut out for farming after all. He had written many little plays for us to act out at home and he always had his head in a book. When he finished the primary school, my parents decided that maybe he should get a year or two in the Christian Brothers' School in Mitchelstown. It was eight miles away and John had to cycle every day. Except he didn't go every single day! Sometimes, the thought of that long journey, seemed too depressing, and he mitched, spending his time reading, in some old disused house or barn. We pretended that we thought he had a romantic rendezvous with the daughter of the farmer who owned the barn! That didn't go down too well with John, who was rather shy with girls!. The teachers finally arrived out to our house to find out why he wasn't in school and all hell broke loose. They knew he had ability and didn't want him to throw away his chances. In fact, the day of the Leaving Cert. Exam, the Brothers sent out a car to make sure he'd sit the examination! Many of our friends and neighbours thought my father was mad to send his only son to school, but my father knew that he wouldn't be happy on the land.

John was very proud of our father's involvement in the War of Independence and never tired of listening to the stories he told of his escapades. He got scholarships to various Irish colleges in the summers of the early fifties (including Newcastle and Glenageary) and also spent a year in the Albert Agricultural College in Dublin. Eventually, he trained as a forester and, after spending some time in different parts of the country, he settled down in Enniscorthy, Co. Wexford with his wife, Rosalleen, and their three children.

Here was a good, kind and generous brother, who had no hesitation in helping around the house when called upon. We accepted without question that he was our mother's pet but he never took advantage of it. He often dried the dishes for me and would polish our shoes for Sunday Mass. The only time he dug in his heels was when we asked him to drive us to dances. My mother would have had no problem in letting us go out if we had a big brother to watch over us. However, he protested that he didn't know how to dance and had no interest in learning. I gave him a few lessons but he never got the hang of it. I gave him a few driving lessons as well!

John and Dara

John is a shy, modest person who likes the simple things of life. He still has a passion for writing and wrote several books in both Irish and English over the years. He has published a series of books 'as gaeilge', which are on the curriculum in many of the Gaelscoileanna.

I think my parents were very far-sighted to give him the chance to go to school rather than pressurising him to stay on the land, as parents of previous generations did. He certainly earned their respect, though his life took a different direction and he didn't become the son and heir to the Kearney estate after all!

CYCLING TO SCHOOL

Blaring alarm clocks, dark mornings, wet clothes and cross nuns. The long eight-mile cycle drained all ambition and enthusiasm. I was always late!

It was fixed that I would go to the secondary school in town, so my father bought me a new Raleigh bicycle to travel the eight-mile journey. I was a little bit excited about the bike, as I'd never before owned anything vaguely valuable. I learned how to pump the wheels, and mend punctures, with the little repair kit, which was attached to the back of the saddle.

Making time in the mornings was a nightmare. There was no mollycoddling then and you had to put yourself out to school. As I jumped, shivering, from my bed, I might hear the rain coming down in bucketfuls outside. Lighting the fire or primus stove to boil the kettle, or maybe even going to the river for water was far too much trouble. I usually took off without any breakfast. Despite having two alarm clocks to wake me up, I hardly ever managed to be on time. I remember that on my school report card I always got HOPELESS for punctuality. I blamed the bicycle for my lateness, saying I got punctures. One nun suggested I get a new bike. The sisters, in those times, never moved outside the gates of their convent, so they had little understanding or sympathy for the long journeys that girls, like me, had to travel to school, sometimes in the dark.

It was a dreary prospect on a frosty winter's morning to get ready for school and set off for Mitchelstown. I suppose I wasn't very motivated, even though, at the back of my mind, I realised that I was probably lucky to get the chance of secondary education. It was rare enough in those days. My mother had cut down a black dress of her own to make my uniform so when it was accessorised with white collar and belt I looked like a small nun! The worst part was the homemade black knitted stockings held up by garters, which dug into my legs.

The school day passed happily in the rarefied confines of the convent. Up to this, we had been accustomed to being pushed and elbowed around by the boys, so being with girls only created a gentler environment. Our English teacher, Sr. Patrick was a sweet, cultured lady, who nurtured our developing talents with skill and sensitivity. The same couldn't be said of some of the others, who didn't impress at all and almost destroyed our already shaky self-confidence!

There was one in particular, who was less than impressed with my culinary expertise. She went mad one day because there was a black spot on my cookery overall. If she could only realise the trouble it had been to wash and iron that white apron. The triangular stone that had to be reddened in the fire, and then secured in the iron, had accidentally hopped out and created the problem! It was no use trying to explain. Then, I had never heard of rough puff pastry. My mother always made an apple tart with dough. I'd never seen a Brussels sprout, so how could I know how to prepare one. The nun was appalled at my ignorance!

Around this time I saw watches advertised in The Sunday Press for thirty shillings, and I thought how handy it would be if I could check the time as I cycled along. My aunt would come for apples every September and usually she gave me a half-crown when she was leaving. After about a year of scrimping and scraping I had saved enough money. I sent it off to Dores' of Dame Street in Dublin and several weeks later, I was the proud owner of my first watch. It didn't help my punctuality though. Only now I knew just how late I was! We even went to school on Saturday to learn 'plain chant' from Sister Consilio. My father wondered what use this would be to me unless I intended staying in the convent. He had plenty jobs he could put me doing around the farm on Saturdays!

I got three pence every day to get a cup of tea at a restaurant in the town to have with my bread and butter (that's if I bothered bringing any) but I thought spending money on tea would be an awful waste. Barry's had a sweet shop with gobstoppers, strings of liquorice, jelly babies, bull's eyes and conversation lozenges and you could get a lot for a couple of pence. On the other hand, you could get a threepenny ice-cream at the top of the town ...

On fair days, it wasn't easy manoeuvring the bicycle through the dirty streets filled with wild, bellowing cattle. Later when the selling was done, the pubs would be full.

It took us a while to get used to the town girls of whom we were a bit in awe. After all, they had grown up here and could walk around the town as if they owned it! They talked about boys. They were smart and confident. Sure, why wouldn't they? They didn't have the drudgery that we did. Bit by bit, though, we realised that they were just like ourselves and they became our friends. They sometimes resented us country girls, too, because the nuns might comment on our good sense. They thought that we were conscientious and not wild and flighty like town girls. We hadn't the energy to be flighty after the long journey to school.

Going home in the evenings wasn't half as bad, because I had company. Two friends that I'd known in primary school were with me for a good part of the journey and we chatted and acted the fool to shorten the way. I could have had them in the mornings too if I'd got up on time! Sometimes, we cycled three abreast and our bikes got entangled and we fell off and landed in the ditch. A few cuts and bruises never bothered us. The roads were quiet anyway, so there wasn't much real danger of being hurt.

I had an aunt, a returned Yank, who was a hairdresser, living in the town, beside the school. My mother wanted me to stay with her to cut out the eight-mile journey. I almost considered being a town girl. However, because she was a spinster with very weird ideas about how children should behave, I didn't relish being her lodger. The few times I did stay with her, she had me up at the crack of dawn, listening to the birds singing, praying and going to Mass. The long cycle was preferable to listening to her advice about how I could be improved.

One of the highlights of my time at this school was when a troupe of travelling players performed Hamlet for us. It was my first experience of Shakespeare. It was memorable and I remember coming back on my bicycle almost in a trance. The powerful speeches and passages were going round in my head, though I didn't understand them.

My bike came to a bad end. One morning, I got up earlier than usual and decided to go up a narrow short cut that connected to the main road to meet my friend, Mary, so we could cycle to school together. A neighbour was driving his creamery cart towards me but he was looking behind him! I quickly dismounted, threw the bike up on the ditch and ran for safety. The bike slid down on the road again and the creamery cart drove over it and flattened it. My parents weren't too happy and, of course, blamed me rather than the neighbour.

'If you'd gone the road you were supposed to be on, it would never have happened,' said my mother crossly.

Anyway, as luck would have it the school year was almost finished so I managed to get to school for the last few weeks. After that mother said I was going to boarding school. But that's a whole other story!

A LUCKY WOMAN

I can still picture Mossie: sprightly, middle-aged as he bends over the horse's tackling. He nimbly works the packing needle with the waxed hemp through the leather. Sleeves rolled up, shoe-laces open. The sheepdog sprawled in front of the fire beside him.

And Bridie, a little ball of a woman, the red marks from the Wellingtons showing below her knees. Bright, inquisitive eyes blinking a welcome from behind her glasses.

We were drawn like magnets to this love nest in the middle of the fields which to-day is only a heap of stones . . .

'Would you have any fellow over your way, that would suit our Bridie?' Tom Flynn smiled, half joking, wholly in earnest, as he handed my father his twenty Sweet Afton cigarettes. It was during the war and cigarettes were rationed. Father was a regular customer to this particular shop.

Tom Flynn's sister, Bridie, was a dumpy little woman on the wrong side of forty. She had a spread on her like a hatching hen! Her bright eyes, behind the glasses, constantly blinked questioningly at you. Because she loved reading, sometimes exchanging books with my mother, she was an interesting conversationalist. She was also a great favourite with us children, because she never spoke down to us.

Bridie had spent many years working in England, cooking in rich houses, but had recently returned to nurse her sick mother. When the old lady passed away, she was at a loose end and on the look out! The local priest had commended her for her daughterly devotion and given her great hope when he told her, 'You did a good thing there, Bridie. You'll be very lucky yet.

Anyway, my father brought 'the word' to our neighbour Mossie Maloney the following week. A fresh forty-five, Mossie had lived alone since the death of his parents. Of medium height and wiry build, Mossie had a slightly malicious streak when it came to local scandals. You could say that he regulated the morals of the young ones because they feared the rumours he might spread about them! Apart from that he was funny, good-humoured and popular.

He was nice to us and in the autumn could magic apples out of his pockets like a conjuror when he came for his weekly card game. When my father told Mossie the good news of the possible match, he was chuffed as could be. He still harboured romantic notions. Wouldn't a woman be terribly handy about the place for cooking and making the bed? Meetings were arranged, the dowry fixed and a date set.

'Would she breed?' Mossie asked my father. They would have made wonderful parents but sadly the marriage was childless. His house was set in the middle of the fields. There was no road access, except by a path over a ditch or down the river by horse and cart. This was his creamery route. The water level wouldn't be very high of course, except in a flood, but wouldn't you wonder how the wheels of the cart stood up to the rough terrain. In later years, a neighbour built a gravelled passage, adjacent to Mossie's house and would allow him to use it but he refused.

'The river was good enough for my parents and 'twill do me too.'

So that was how his new bride was transported to her new home – up the river by horse and cart. She wasn't complaining. She was well pleased with her new man.

She needed to be! Mossie's house was a tumble-down, two-roomed thatched shack, badly in need of repair. Inside, the kitchen ceiling was a maze of knotted and knarled branches blackened with age and smoke. The sunlight barely penetrated the tiny kitchen window where the only furniture was a rickety table and a pair of sagging sugán chairs. A big black crane dominated the sooty fireplace from which hung a pot and a kettle.

The bedroom was no better – dingy and murky with years of cobwebs trailing from the ceiling and around the holy picture. An old iron bed stood in the corner, over which was draped a pair of socks rigid with dirt and a rosary beads. Bridie looked around her.

'There's work to be done here, Mossie,' she sighed, taking off her wedding finery and knuckling down to business.

And the house wasn't the only thing that needed an overhaul. Bridie set about introducing a few house rules.

'Leave those dirty Wellingtons outside the door. I don't want muck and clay all over the house,' she'd scold crossly.

'When my mother was alive she never minded!'

'Well I mind,' retorted Bridie, 'and while we're at it, I wish you'd stop slurping your tea out of the saucer at supper time and spitting into the fire! No one does the like of that nowadays.

'Does she want me to scald meself with the hot tay?' Mossie half sniggered to himself. 'Or maybe she'll have me wearing bedroom slippers around the house next!'

But this was only friendly domestic banter. Bridie and Mossie were as close as two peas in a pod and lived and worked happily side by side. Each morning, for thirty odd years, they rose at cockcrow, tackled the horse and cart and travelled over the fields to milk their four cows. While Mossie took the milk to the creamery, Bridie fed the calves and hens. She'd have a nice fresh egg boiled for her husband's breakfast, when he returned with all the juicy gossip.

'Young McGrath was caught without ere a light on his bike, coming back from the hall, and hadn't he Maurice Dolan's young one up on the cross bar. What do you think of that? Old Josie Murphy had the priest last night. I heard that she looked a bit shook with a while all right and had a dangerous bad cough. And oh, didn't Jerry Conlan win the goose at Gorman's gamble!'

Mossie basked in Bridie's undivided attention as he finished his egg. She had her arms folded and her two eyes fixed on him as he related all the news.

'Is Tim Delaney back at the creamery yet or is he still bad in the bed, Mossie? And did you hear if Jack McGrath's daughter went back to England?

Bridie wanted all the news. She was a great listener and a good cook, too, and delighted in preparing appetising meals insofar as the limited facilities allowed. Having cooked for strangers in England, it was nice to have your own man to fuss over. She did her best with the house, but the smoke defied all her decorating efforts. Mossie was reluctant to spend money on improvements. Sure, wasn't their bit of money better off safe and secure in the bank? Bridie read her novels by the fire at night and would recite interesting passages for Mossie.

'But did that really happen?' he'd enquire.

'Ah no, Mossie, sure 'tis a story.'

'Arrah, Bridie, don't be wasting my time. Don't you know I've no time for them made up yarns.'

Getting to Mass and town was difficult, but neighbours helped out. Bridie and Mossie got full enjoyment out of a day's shopping, meeting friends and relations. Mossie would wait in the pub while Bridie bought women's things in the local drapers. But how they loved coming back to their sequestered haven in the middle of the fields! This was where they were truly happy. Bridie would smile to herself, recalling the priest's prophetic words. She was indeed a lucky woman, happy and content with her lot. They had to scramble over ditches and squeeze through hedges on their journey to our house to play cards. They loved the game, but hated losing! The neighbours prevailed on them to eventually invest in a television and get all the world news. It was a novelty for a short time, but Mossie preferred the local gossip!

When Bridie died suddenly one night, the priest and doctor had terrible trouble finding the house. The undertaker had an even bigger dilemma. The neighbour who owned the adjacent passage, suggested using it as a funeral route but Mossie was adamant.

'She came up the river the first day. She'll go out the same way.'

So Bridie's coffin rattled and shook over rocks and stones on her last trip down the river. I could imagine her chuckle of approval. Mossie was no use without her. He lived for only a few short years, and the place is now empty and deserted. Despite the absence of material comforts and luxuries, they stand out in my mind, as a truly happy, united couple.

The old house is just a heap of stones now, almost reclaimed by nature. All that remains are the echoes of happier times.

OUR FIRST CAR

It was something we'd dreamt about. A car of our own! We memorised our registration number immediately, as well as dozens of other cars around us. Being in from the weather was like heaven, after being frozen and drenched in the horse and trap.

Nancy, the horse, disgraced herself when she bolted, coming back from Mass one Sunday, in the early fifties. We were all dumped unceremoniously out on the road as the trap turned upside-down. My sister's main worry was that the buckle on her new patent shoes was broken, and she was performing in a school concert in Ballyporeen that night! Dolly, the mare was getting past it and now that we couldn't fully trust Nancy any more, my father made a momentous decision. He would invest in his very first motor car. The question of a car had come up from time to time before, when our neighbour, Jack, came to visit. He described all the advantages.

'Johnny, you won't know yourself! Think of the comfort and convenience of sitting into your car, in your own yard, and driving at your ease to Clonmel or Thurles to your meetings. No more waiting for buses or lifts, snug and cosy and in out of the weather.'

My father would be all fired up after Jack's visits and my mother and he would be chatting about it around the fire after we were gone to bed. We heard everything of course! Since he was a member of Tipperary County Council, he was often on the road and a car would definitely be handy, they decided. The moment had come.

A deal was made with his friend, Garret, from Cahir, and a little black secondhand Ford car (registration number IH 6707) became part of the family. With typically bad timing, I was in bed with whooping cough when it arrived and had to be content with admiring it through the window. What a thrill! It represented luxury, freedom and travel. To God knows where.

When I recovered, you can bet that I investigated the car from top to bottom. It had brown leather seats and a running board for getting in. Two yellow arrows, situated one on each side of the car, shot out when you indicated. The choke and starter were pulled to get the engine going or, failing that, you cranked it with a starting handle.

Having airily dumped Dolly now that we had a new mode of transport, we sheepishly had to beg forgiveness when the car refused to start. How often was the old mare called out of retirement, tackled and hitched to the front of the stubborn car. She set off at a trot, with Dad at the steering wheel. Fine precision and judgment were needed, when the engine fired, to stop the car driving over Dolly!

If all else failed, we called on our mechanic friend, Walter, to investigate matters under the bonnet. The only trouble here was that Walter was a melodeon player. He and my father might strike up a session of music and the car was often forgotten. You wouldn't want to have your hat and coat on waiting to go on a journey!

Our first car had no heater, radio or seat belts. Petrol was 12p a gallon and a driving licence cost 30 shillings. Anyone who presented himself to the Tax Offices with the money could get tax cover with a minimum of form filling. Most byroads were rough and pot-holed then, so there were a lot of punctures. We always allowed extra time on a journey for changing tyres!

Anyway, my father was delighted with his car and the next few weeks saw him, dementedly, driving in and out between two posts in the big field, where he couldn't do too much damage. Jack made encouraging noises from the sideline.

'Back away Johnny, steady now, hether a small bit more. STOP!'

What Dad lacked in driving skills, was more than compensated by his enthusiasm and oneness with the car. He took to it like a duck to water. We now went to Mass in style. Gone was the rounding up of the horse on Sunday morning or brushing off hairs before going into the church. Gone was the misery of sitting for an hour in the trap on a wet or frosty day. Going to town was a joy. The weather no longer mattered. We had access to Woolworth's – an Aladdin's Cave of treasures, situated in Clonmel. Our carefully hoarded pennies, extracted from our parents playing Ludo, were gladly exchanged for pencils, books and sweets. It was magic. We would then make our way to our cousin, Maggie Sargent, who had a shop on the narrow street, for a cup of tea. There might be a purchase of fresh meat, wrapped in brown paper, and tied with twine, for tomorrow's dinner. The paper was often blood-stained by the time we got it home!

The little car took us to other villages, strange towns and we visited long lost relations and friends who had been inaccessible up to this. Even going for a drive, without any definite destination in mind, was a novelty for a while. The car also took the churns of milk to the creamery now, so Nancy and Dolly were made redundant. I went to the seaside for the first time. I had heard of people going on pioneer excursions to Tramore but here I was at last, looking out at the great expanse of water. It was beyond my wildest imaginings. Mother brought a flask of tea and sandwiches, which we ate on the beach. I ran in and out of the sea excitedly, and Dad took our pictures on the old Brownie camera.

Our little car often went to Barry's garage in Cahir for repairs, where my father had a very cordial relationship with the owner. People were very loyal to shops and business premises that time and Dad wouldn't dream of going anywhere else.

When my mother finally decided to take her first driving lesson, she was advised to begin by adjusting her rear view mirror. She took one look and shrieked in dismay

'Oh, good gracious, my hair is a show. I must go in and comb it.'

This ended my mother's driving career, before it had even started. She was much too nervous to take the wheel anyway. She was scared enough with my father, too, I'm afraid, and she put more faith in the Lord than in my father's driving prowess. She was especially nervous going up and down steep hills and the Sacred Heart was often called on to get us home safely.

They drove to town one market day, up to the top of the square, which sloped down to the main street. My father went into the post office, leaving my mother alone in the car. When she suddenly noticed it moving, not hesitating, she nimbly jumped to safety and watched as it proceeded down through the busy thoroughfare, miraculously avoiding people and animals, coming to a halt at the bottom without doing any damage.

'Why the dickens didn't you put your foot on the pedal or pull the handbrake?' demanded my puzzled father when he emerged from the post office.

'How was I supposed to know where them things were located?' replied my unrepentant mother. It was obvious that she had no interest in the workings of the car.

There was no speed limit in the fifties and my father drove along happily in the middle of the road, smoking his cigarette, only taking evasive action if he spotted another car. It must be said that he wasn't the best driver in the world! The traffic was light so, happily, accidents rarely occurred. Sadly, he lost the sight of one eye, but maintained that his sight was better in the car than anywhere else. It's worth mentioning that car horns were regularly blown back then, going around corners or passing people, cattle, donkeys, horses or ducks on the road. When our horn went on the blink, my resourceful father suggested that I go along and sound a horn-like note on the accordion as necessary. I was delighted, to oblige! He would let me practice driving from the age of fourteen, coming back from town, his only proviso being, 'Don't tell your mother!'

Thanks to him, I had plenty of experience and confidence by the time I got my first license at eighteen.

Our first new car – a Ford Anglia (reg. EHI 504) arrived about that time, and I was as proud as punch to be allowed to drive it. My sisters and I motored to lots of dances. They had the money for petrol and I had the driving license! We were cautioned to be very careful. One night, however, I broke a front light, as I was stopping, at the stage in Kilcoran. The stage was a big wooden floor situated in a shady spot beside a shop on the main Cork–Dublin road and people congregated here during the summer months to dance. The music was provided by a great local accordion player, Seanie Cunningham, who

Our first new car – Ann driving

had no microphone or amplification of any kind, so it was hard work to be heard above the noise of the traffic and talk. That particular night I had begged my father to give us the car. We would be in big trouble if he thought we'd broken anything, so we had to get up early next morning and make some excuse, so we could go to the garage to get it fixed without our parents' knowledge. I'd never drive again if they found out. And they never did!

Yanks came to visit that summer and I was detailed to drive to Shannon, with father in the passenger seat. He wondered if I would be able to manage the new traffic lights in Limerick! I remember his big worry was that my aunt would kiss him. He hadn't seen her for thirty-five years!

The thrill and novelty of driving cars is long gone. There are several cars to every household nowadays. I doubt that they would have much patience with one, like ours, that sometimes refused to start! Cars may come and go but the old Ford model that opened up my world will always hold a special place in my heart. It was truly a worthy successor to Dolly.

GOING PLACES

*'Where will we go while I have the good suit on?' my father would ask
on a Sunday afternoon. Now that we had a car, we were rearing to go.
Somewhere, anywhere! But we couldn't go too far as Dad didn't like night
driving. But one time we took a chance . . .*

Owning a motorcar was very exciting. In theory, we could
go anywhere now. Once we had enough petrol in the tank!
In practice, however, it was a different matter. How often had we
dolled ourselves up – my mother with her hat on, my father newly
shaven – all of us sitting in the car ready for the off, but the blooming
thing wouldn't start. In spite of using the choke, the starting handle,
prayers and curses, there wasn't a geek. Happily, this wasn't always the
case. We started by exploring the small neighbouring towns, Cahir,
Mitchelstown, Cashel, Clonmel and even Thurles in our little car.
Then, one time, we ventured further afield.

My eldest sister, Kathleen, was in Mary Immaculate College in
Limerick, training to become a primary teacher. Conditions were
strict there, almost like her previous boarding school. She didn't get
home very often. On one occasion, she wrote to my mother with
the news that the College was holding a pageant in which she was
taking part and she'd love if we could come.

I wondered what a pageant was. My mother decided it was some
sort of a play and she was well-accustomed to attending those in
the local hall. After some discussion, my father made a momentous
decision. He would drive to Limerick, which was some forty miles
away, and we'd make a night of it. I'd never been in a city and I was
thrilled at the prospect of the trip. My mother put on her best navy
costume with matching shoes. My father wore his Sunday suit with a

collar and tie and his hat. His peaked cap was for every day use. I had to be content with my school coat and my new furry brown boots.

We set off early so we would have the light, one way, at least. Dad drove in his usual leisurely manner, mostly in the middle of the road, admiring all the houses and fields of cows as we passed. He wasn't very accustomed to night driving so this would be a major challenge. Mam was nervous and gave out the rosary to be on the safe side!

Kathleen was delighted to see us and showed us around the college and we met some of the nuns. Later, we all trooped into the big hall and waited expectantly. We immediately picked out Kathleen, resplendent in her long dress and bonnet, singing with a group of other students. It was a type of religious musical, specially arranged by the nuns for the Marian Year.

Having taken our leave of Kathleen, we headed for home. The traffic on the road was light and we made good headway. However, about half way through our journey a bad fog came down. Now, we were in a pucker. My father completely lost his bearings. Everything was shrouded in mist and we could barely see the road. My mother started praying. My father stopped the car and lit a cigarette.

'Is that the shape of a house there to the left?' he said, starting up the car again.

'The Lord save us, Johnny, be careful!' said my mother hysterically.

My father drove very slowly into the farmer's yard, turned off the engine and knocked at the door of the house.

'God bless all here,' he murmured as a surprised woman opened the door. It must have been about 11.30 p.m.

'We're lost in the fog,' explained my father. 'We're coming from Limerick and we're not sure where we are.'

'You're just outside Knocklong,' said the woman in a friendly voice. 'Come in out of the cold, let ye and I'll put on the kettle. 'Tis a terrible night.'

We stayed for about two hours, drinking tea and chatting to the woman and her husband. They made connections about people and places that they both knew and the fog was cleared when we got back on the road.

Kathleen was to be the reason also for our next big journey. When she qualified as a teacher, her first position was in Dublin. She was staying, temporarily, with a niece of my mother's until she found her feet. Coming up to Christmas, she suggested that we all pay a visit to 'The Big Smoke' when everything would be grand and festive. John and Eileen were away, so it was just my parents and I at home.

My father considered that he wasn't equipped to drive the long journey to Dublin on his own. He called on our good friend and neighbour Walter, who dropped everything, to accommodate us. He loved cars anyway and was game for the adventure. Walter, my parents and myself set off in high glee for our great adventure. I clearly remember that somewhere round the Curragh, we were all singing 'Doonaree' which was the pop song of the day. My father and Walter were tracing and swopping stories and we never felt the journey. We stopped at the 'Red Cow' for tea and I saw my first jukebox!

Kathleen and my cousin were delighted to see us, though it must have been a tight squeeze for her to fit us all. Eileen, our cousin had a young family of her own. We went to the cinema that night to see a film called 'Genevieve' which, fittingly, was about an old car. Next day, we joined the crowds of people walking up and down O'Connell Street. I asked Dad if there would be that number of people on the streets every day or was it just coming up to Christmas. He assured me that the place was thronged at all times, Sunday and Monday. Where were they all going? I couldn't believe it! I worried that the big, green double-decker buses might topple over on top of us as they screeched up and down O'Connell Street.

'What's that big yoke sticking up in the air?' I wanted to know as I craned my neck skywards.

'Oh, that's Nelson's Pillar,' answered my father. 'Though I don't know what in the name of God the likes of him is doing decorating the centre of our capital city. Sure, isn't he an Englishman!'

We moved on to Henry Street, which was twinkling with fairy lights. The old women, with their stalls in Moore Street, were shouting, 'Get the last of the Cheeky Charlies!'

Our mother and father with Ann on O'Connell Street.

I was star struck with the shiny, brightly coloured balloons and decorations, moving Santas and cribs in the shop windows. I had never seen anything like it. My father was admiring watches in jewellery shops, longing for a wrist model rather than the pocket watch he had all his life. Kathleen surprised him. Before we left, she produced a beautiful wristwatch from a box, which she had been saving for his Christmas present. He was as delighted as a child. We had our picture taken in O'Connell Street, and after the photographer had laboriously spelt out my father's address, Coolagarranroe, he enquired how many copies Dad wanted. My father said that he didn't want any!

However, I still have that old photograph recording our visit to the big city, so, it seems we must have got one after all! As we travelled back, past the Curragh, Portlaoise and 'The Horse and Jockey', I was quiet as I went over everything in my head. There was a big world out there and our little car was helping us to explore it!

BOARDING SCHOOL REVISITED

I can still taste those Sunday sausages. Leftovers were divided out on a strict rota system, so you waited weeks for that extra one. Another magic moment was Sr. Angela holding up a letter with your name on it!

I have a recurring dream. I'm back in my old boarding school, searching frantically for my wash-place in the long corridor where rows of white basins stretch endlessly. But I can't find mine. Then, I realise that I am an adult, horribly out of place amongst a crowd of schoolgirls. Thankfully, I wake up, but all the old feelings and memories of that time come flooding back . . .

Having cycled eight miles to the local school for two years and been soaked, exhausted, and frost bitten, I jumped at my mother's suggestion of going to boarding school. Whether it improved my lot (or me!) is debatable, because this brought its own set of problems. It certainly gave me a valuable insight into the day-to-day workings of a convent at that time, if I had any notion of entering, and allowed me to stand on my own two feet.

The school was some ten miles from my home and was run with military-like precision by the Mercy nuns. They boasted an excellent reputation for producing top-class students, who brought honour to themselves and the school. Their photographs, with a list of achievements, confronted us challengingly from the wall near the cloakroom, as we changed our shoes. My sister Kathleen's picture was among them and this only added to my misery because I feared it was useless to try to measure up. Having had two older sisters who had boarded at the same school already, I wasn't expecting a holiday camp. Still, nothing prepared me for the shock of all the petty rules and regulations. Up to this, I had been as free as a bird, living on a farm where the pace of life was leisurely. There was no fixed times for doing anything, except perhaps milking the cows and going to the creamery.

But it was all different now. Breaking the school rules meant a fine of half-a-crown, so we were very careful to avoid talking after lights out at night, or being caught with outdoor shoes in the refectory. Our uniform was woefully drab, being predominantly navy blue, accessorised by long black stockings. When we ventured out for walks through the town, the local boys would, jeeringly, shout 'black beetles' after us! Of course, there were a few girls on whom even a shapeless school uniform looked well. Sadly, this was not so in my case. I inherited various bits and pieces from my sisters, who were different in shape and size to me. The navy all-purpose gabardine coat, with assorted patches, comes to mind as being particularly hideous. It hung way below my ankles. I was supposed to grow into it at some stage, but this, unfortunately, never happened.

A dressing gown was another piece of clothing with which we weren't familiar. Mine was made from a discarded, pink coat and looked quite nice and cosy when my mother had finished altering it, changing the buttons and putting braid around the collar. Because we washed every morning in a draughty corridor, we certainly needed it.

Cold, dreary, winter days invariably take me back to boarding school, when our hands ached with chilblains and our hearts with misery and despair. The first night back was awful, and you could hear muffled sobs coming from various corners of the dormitory. It seemed like an eternity to the Christmas holidays and some girls, away from home for the very first time, were understandably very homesick. Others were made of sterner stuff and seemed to take it in their stride. We were all envious as we listened to one Cork girl recounting her romantic, summer rendezvous with some boy. I didn't dare mention that I'd spent my summer thinning turnips and saving hay!

'Everybody up!'

The sister-in-charge floated through the dormitory, ringing the big iron bell, chasing everybody out of bed. Then, it was off to our allotted places in the long corridor, where we washed hands, faces and chattering teeth from basins of cold water.

We were dressed and in church for 7 a.m Mass every morning, without exception. Unless we were literally dying! Complaining of being sick meant a dose of castor oil, which was considered the cure-all, so you thought long and hard before you complained. The sticky grey slimy porridge, which appeared every morning for breakfast, was highly suspect, but refusing to eat it was not an option. The tea came in huge aluminium teapots with the milk and sugar already mixed in. I remember how amazed I was, when I went home for the first school holidays, to see black tea coming from the pot. We also considered that the ceiling, table and chairs were very low and doll's house-like, compared to the spacious dormitories and lengthy corridors in school.

Before the school day began, we each had to do 'a charge'. This meant being responsible for cleaning or dusting a particular area of the boarding quarters. On completion, it was duly inspected. We must have saved the nuns a packet on housekeeping bills. Anyway, there was a frantic scramble every morning after breakfast to get to the broom closet to get the best brushes. Not being as highly motivated as others in the cleaning department, I was often left with a hairless excuse for a brush for which no amount of elbow grease could compensate. This could result in me being late for class and getting told off.

By and large, I enjoyed the school day, although one particular teacher put the fear of God into me, often reducing me to tears. In her own way, she had our interests at heart, but her methods were daunting. Algebra and geometry were a complete mystery to me, particularly as we did everything through Irish. I must say, however, that I enjoyed the English and Irish classes. Our teacher was a gentle, refined nun who encouraged in us a love of Shakespeare, Milton and Shelley. She nurtured our small seeds of talent and urged us always to aspire to greatness.

'Hitch your wagons to a star, girls,' she would chant.

'I wonder what cover up they have used to-day?' moaned my friend Mary, throwing her eyes to heaven, as we trooped into the refectory for our lunch. The same tasteless meat was recycled for the week, appearing in the guise of white hash on Monday and as brown hash or shepherd's pie on following days. For some reason, we always went home to our parents looking fat and healthy, so it can't have been that bad. The monotony and predictability of our diet was the worst. Even a pot of homemade jam, sent in the post, was a treat.

We were strictly supervised in the study hall each evening by various sisters. They watched like hawks for idling or note passing between the girls. If the notes were confiscated and anything of a suspicious nature was discovered, it meant trouble. The punishment for writing to a boy, in those times, was expulsion. Boys were bad news! We enjoyed twenty minutes of dancing to records in the recreation hall before we went to bed. This helped to warm us up for the cold night ahead in the freezing dormitory. It was here that I learned to do the waltz, quickstep and tango with my friends. It came in more useful later on than a lot of the other stuff I studied!

And so to bed! But I never warmed up properly in the winter. As I lay awake, shivering, all my worries reared their ugly heads. I went over my geography one last time. I wondered if I would get money from home soon to keep my creditors off my back. Would I ever match the achievements of my sisters, with whom I was constantly being compared?

We had a half-day from school on Saturdays, so this was the time for further housekeeping chores. We had an extended 'charge' to attend to, as well as our own bits and pieces, like polishing shoes, sorting laundry and doing any necessary mending or sewing. It was also Confession day. Since we had to go to the parish church, which adjoined the convent, we were able to mingle with penitents from the outside world. It's hard to know what the priest made of our mutterings and stuttering about things that weren't even remotely sinful. He corrected my grammar one day!

Then a Retreat priest came and introduced us to BAD THOUGHTS. From then on, we all had at least one decent sin. Even in our confined state, he explained, we were probably committing loads of mortal sins. In our minds. Thinking about boys!

My sexual urges were buried deep under layers of other, more pressing needs, like hunger, homesickness and solving my geometry problems! I would have been much more likely to have had orgasmic fantasies about a good feed of bacon and cabbage than any pimply-faced young fellow. The only men we saw on a regular basis were the priest who said Mass each morning and Denis, the elderly convent handyman. We were well out of harm's way!

Every Saturday night in the study hall, we were subjected to a religious 'pep-talk' from one of the sisters. She reminded us to always behave in a ladylike manner, as our bodies were the temples of the Holy Spirit.

'You have to set a high standard, girls,' she told us, 'as boys have no control over their lust. Remind them to keep God's holy commandments and to show respect for you at all times.'

They were getting more interesting by the minute, these crazed, passion-filled, members of the opposite sex. The ones I'd seen around at home had seemed rather ordinary and dull. We were told to make the Mass the centre of our lives

'If you were on your knees 'til you died and you lived to be ninety, you couldn't make up for one holy Mass'.

This was what the holy nun told us, and it must have made an impression, since I remember it clearly all those years later. She also emphasised the sacrifices our parents were making by putting us in boarding school in the first place, and what a sin it would be, on our part, if we didn't make the most of our opportunities. We were expected to make a visit to the church every day between 1.15 and 1.30. And we even had special little prayer books to read. Sometimes I tried to sneak in my history book instead, to revise for the next class. The sisters certainly did their utmost to transmit their strong Catholic faith to us. It's only now, in retrospect, that we appreciate how hard they worked on our behalf.

These nuns were feminists, though the women's liberation movement hadn't officially been declared yet. They were strong, resourceful women, who constantly tried to make us see the value of a good education, which would enable us, one day, to take our place in the world. They exerted an extraordinary influence, not only on us, but also on our parents who thought they could do no wrong! Despite having a demure appearance, we realised that they were formidable little women, who had their own preferences and political leanings like everybody else. We noticed the nuns who got on well and the ones who barely tolerated each other!

After lunch on Sundays, we lined up in twos for our three-mile walk, with the nuns bringing up the rear. Depending on which road we went, we might see a familiar face, which unleashed all our longings for home. We enviously observed parents and children out together, chatting and laughing, and teenagers cavorting freely down by the river. I was only allowed visitors on one Sunday of each term, so home receded further and further from my consciousness.

Sunday was bath day and also our day for writing letters. All incoming and outgoing letters were carefully vetted, so you certainly weren't going to pour your heart out. It was a rather stilted few lines, with dull comments about school, that our parents received each Tuesday. There might also be a request for money and when this duly arrived, the nun took it out of the envelope. You had to tell her what you wanted to buy with it before she gave you back your own money!

On some Sundays and special feast days, we were shown the popular films of the day, like *The Student Prince, Rommel, the Desert Fox, High Noon* (starring Grace Kelly) and *Desert Song*. Our cinematographer, one of the sisters, was an ardent film buff, and if you could get her talking about films during our Irish class, she would get carried away and forget to check the homework! She shaded the more daring love scenes in the film with her hand. When we complained about this, she apologised and said she was doing it because of the nuns, who would be also watching. These films provided a few magical hours of much needed escape for our poor, famished hearts.

The fire escape, which led from one of the dormitories to the convent grounds below, was a constant source of temptation to the more adventurous-minded. One girl was expelled for risking a trip down its tortuous steps to meet a boy. There was no way I would have dared, especially if boys were as dangerous as the nuns said! Secretly, though, we admired these 'bold' girls who had the nerve to flout the system and we wished we could be like them.

The annual retreat created a welcome diversion from the monotony of schoolwork, and we all became madly religious for a few days. We exchanged holy pictures, commemorating the retreat, inscribed with little pious messages and hopes for the future. We walked around the convent grounds, trance-like, saying prayers and aspirations. I wanted to be a martyr, like Maria Goretti. We threw ourselves at the mercy of the young, good-looking Redemptorist priest in confession. Maybe, he would understand all our teenage insecurities. We listened, in fear and trepidation, in the stillness of the night, for a message from the Holy Ghost calling us to be nuns, and breathed a huge sigh of relief when we heard nothing! It would have been relatively easy to take that next step and renounce the world. We were already leading an almost nun-like existence. There were a number of vocations from the classes each year. Bad and all as the picture was that the nuns painted of the dangerous world out there, I decided to chance it. I'd had nearly enough of convent life.

May was a month to be cherished as summer was on its way. We loved singing 'Bring Flowers of the Rarest' as the statue of Our Lady was carried down the covered walk, which stretched from the convent to the school. Emotions were running high now, as the holidays beckoned. It also meant the end of the road for some students. But first, there was THE PICNIC!

This annual excursion to the town reservoir was definitely the highlight of the year for us. We thoroughly enjoyed every minute, starting with the two-mile walk through wooded countryside. The nuns followed by car with all the picnic goodies. Name any destination in the world where someone might imagine all her holiday dreams coming true. It would be nothing compared to our delight and excitement going to this reservoir! It was the complete freedom from school and rules, there by the lake with your friends, on a bright, summer's day. We laughed, skipped and frolicked like spring lambs and then fell exhausted on to the warm grass. The nuns looked on indulgently. We revelled in the simple pleasure of unaccustomed picnic food and lemonade, and dreamt happily of the glorious future that stretched luxuriantly ahead . . .

Ann's sixth year class – Ann is first in the middle row on the right.

Another little oasis in the desert of boarding-school life was the time preceding the Inter and Leaving Certificate Examinations. The non-exam girls had now gone home and we were a small exclusive group to be pampered and fussed over. Conditions improved. We got special little treats and concessions. We even got to know the nuns a little better, realising with something of a shock, that they were human after all! I recall taking myself down to the nuns' summerhouse, one bright May morning to study for the Leaving Cert. and feeling a great sense of happiness. There was a touch of sadness too. My life was about to change forever.

We missed our friends (who came from all over Ireland) who had shared our misery and confidences for so long. We found to our astonishment that we even missed the nuns, who had made all our decisions and often made us feel miserable and inadequate. Although the strict discipline was at an end, we would carry it around in our heads for many years to come. It was almost as though the sister was still standing over our shoulders, watching, directing . . . It was a big adjustment for a crowd of innocent, untried girls, released on an unsuspecting world. We had to stand on our own now and become responsible citizens.

'Weren't the nuns fairly right about the men though?' remarked my friend Mary one night, as we were reminiscing about boarding school.

'Most lads were certainly very fuzzy about the commandments anyway,' I laughed.

The Spartan regime did us no harm either and only served to heighten our appreciation of good food and other luxuries later on. These nuns took a huge, personal interest in their girls. No teacher today would have the time or energy to devote to pupils that was lavished on us. In those times, parents stayed firmly in the background where their children's education was concerned. They never got involved in subject choices or parent/teacher discussions. Your fate was largely left for the nuns to decide, and their wisdom and authority was never questioned. They decided which career would be most suitable for you, having taken family circumstances etc. into account. Parents and students just quietly acquiesced.

Our social horizons were considerably broadened as, up to this, we had only encountered girls from our own parish at home. Here, we met girls from Dublin, Cork and Kerry. Boarding school made us appreciate our female uniqueness, regarding emotions and feelings and how necessary we were, to balance a world run by men. We learned an enormous amount from each other and we valued our friendships, using them as the foundation on which all our later relationships were built. What a debt of gratitude we owe to our far-seeing parents for making such an enormous sacrifice at a time when money was very scarce. Let's hope we justified their investment in us.

The boarding school is gone now. Nuns are no longer teaching in the modern comprehensive school in the town that caters to both boys and girls. That long corridor that we cleaned and polished and slid down so often is silent. It will never more resound to girlish laughter.

Except, perhaps, in my dreams.

GOING HOME

Home and Christmas are synonymous. It conjures up a roaring fire with the family gathered round playing cards. Coming from the austere regimentation of boarding school, home, for me, took on a more fundamental meaning, like wearing normal clothes, getting enough to eat and staying in bed late.

The countdown had begun a month before. On the calendar beside my bed, I had deliberately, ruthlessly, irrevocably blacked out each passing day. I saved this pleasure until nighttime, just before I went to sleep, so that I could ponder, and possibly dream, about the times that lay ahead. But first there were the Christmas examinations to be got through. Tomorrow I had history and knowing that particular teacher's propensity for long, convoluted questions, I had my work cut out. I would probably end up with writer's cramp if I were lucky.

The weather was seasonably cold and we shivered as we washed in ice-cold water, from basins in the long corridor, dressing gowns wrapped tightly. How different the picture would be in a few short weeks, when the blazing turf fire would warm the cockles of my heart and cast bright, gleaming shadows on the strands of holly criss-crossing the kitchen ceiling.

And so we trooped to the refectory where grey, slimy porridge awaited us. Oh, how I wished for that Christmas goose, with all the trimmings and Mother's delicious potato stuffing. She would have it cooking for hours, the smell permeating the whole house. The jelly would be left to set on the parlour table – away from my brother's greedy eyes!

After breakfast, we lined up for Mass in the small Convent chapel, holding our black, leather-covered missals with cold, chilblained fingers. We had the coloured ribbons to guide us through epistles and gospels. But our hearts and minds were miles away. I had so many worries. Would I know my history? Would I escape criticism and humiliation for even one day? Would I get a letter from home, telling me if they were able to collect me on the dot. Surely God would listen to my prayers.

I couldn't wait for Midnight Mass in the church at home, meeting all the neighbours, listening to their warm words of welcome. The small children would be excited and restless, waiting for Santa Claus. The little village choir would break our hearts with their unchanging, evocative Christmas hymns, 'Silent Night' and 'Adeste Fideles'...

The girls were getting excited now, and would congregate in little groups on each other's beds at night to discuss their plans. Some of the seniors might be going to dances on St. Stephen's Night and hoping to meet boys. Others talked of the style they would buy in Cork and how great it would be to be out of uniform.

The tests were finished and the nuns would now be making out our reports. These always arrived during the school holidays. My mother looked first at conduct and application to study, before she read our marks, so it all came out in the wash if you hadn't been good. The nuns were a bit friendlier now, probably glad to be seeing the back of us for a couple of weeks. How we pitied them, having to stay in that same, bleak, environment for the festive season, with all those prayers to say! We wondered if they would have a goose.

I looked at my calendar. There were only three days left. I had written home and instructed them to be there on the dot of one o'clock. We had a 'Bring and Buy' sale on Sunday and I won a huge box of chocolates. How tempted I was to scoff the lot. But then I imagined the look of delight on my mother's face, when I presented the box to her on Christmas Day and the temptation passed. Here was a woman who had saved from September to December, when we were little, to provide a plentiful and exciting Christmas day. A box of chocolates was small repayment.

Mother Catherine took us out to the recreation hall and positioned a long ladder to the balcony overhead. A few of us climbed up and rooted out the suitcases, dropping them, one by one, to the floor below. Nothing was too much trouble now and we never minded the exertion. We were all in such high good humour.

D-Day finally arrived, but there were still chores to be done. The long corridor had to be swept and polished with hard brushes. Sometimes, if the nuns weren't around, we went sliding and skating down its long expanse in a fit of girlish high spirits. All the dormitories had to be cleaned and dusted thoroughly and were then inspected before we were off the hook. Our blankets, quilts and pillows were made into neat parcels and left on our beds. I always envied the sisters who slept together in the bed beside me, and managed to create a huge mound from their combined blankets! Finally, we were given the all-clear. We dragged the suitcases down the stairs with new found energy and I looked for my father's Ford Prefect car. Hurray! There he was with my mother, waiting.

Without a backward glance at the nuns or the convent, I bounded into the car. As we drove out of the town, I admired the tinsel-lined, lit-up shops, with all their Christmas goods on display, and excitedly watched the local shoppers parading the streets, loaded down with bags. Then we were out in the country, the roads glistening with frost. Coming near home, I waved at some of the neighbours. 'They didn't get holidays in the local school yet,' said my mother, 'you're the first.'

'It's cold enough for snow,' remarked my father as he pulled the car into the yard. 'I must bring in a few big blocks for the back of the fire. You'd never know, the card-players might be on.'

Sally, the sheepdog, came running over, tail wagging furiously in recognition.

'Welcome home, love' said my mother, as we went into the familiar holly-decorated kitchen. 'Kathleen and Eileen are coming tomorrow and John on Christmas Eve. Then we'll all be together. I have sausages for the supper. Are you hungry?'

Later, looking out the window at the darkening sky, I prayed for snow. That would make it the best homecoming ever.

BUS RIDE TO FREEDOM

*A taste of the big city – flashing neon signs; crowded streets; Nelson's
Pillar; learning to apply lipstick; exciting, brightly-lit shops, with clothes
displayed on rails; young men and women walking down O'Connell
street in the middle of the broad daylight holding hands!*

I was home from boarding school for the Easter holidays and I was
really fed up. I was withered from praying during the previous five
days of Holy Week and longed for a bit of excitement. The only thing
I'd done that was remotely interesting was playing a game of '45'
with the neighbours. Then we got a letter from Kathleen in Dublin
inviting me up for a few days.

'Can I go Mam, please, please. I'll even bring you back a present,
PLEASE!'

Where I was going to get the money to bring back presents was
another matter!

Anyway, Mother said I could go, but only for a few days, mind, and
I'd better be on my best behaviour. Being used to boarding school
rules, I knew nothing about anything except best behaviour. But who
knows, even I might lose the run of myself in the big city. I dressed
up, packed my suitcase, and here I was at last on the bus to Dublin.
The conductor was friendly. He asked me if I was still in school and
gave me a half-price ticket. Kathleen met me at the station and I was
ready for any excitement that came my way

She had a nice apartment, which she was sharing with a dark-haired
teacher, Eileen, from Kerry. I was squeezed into a makeshift bed, but
what did I care? Kathleen said that she'd made an appointment for the
next day to have our photographs taken together in the city, to mark
the occasion of my visit. I should put on my best dress. I only had one
and it was white. We had our hair styled and we took the big double-

decker bus to the studio. Smiling and posing for the photographer was a new experience for me, but I loved the attention. It turned out to be a great picture of the two of us. Much better than the ones my mother took with the Brownie camera at home. Years later, some boy saw it on the mantelpiece and took it away with him. What a waste!

Anyway, Kathleen took me shopping and introduced me to the magic of the big, bright stores with all the clothes that I couldn't afford, alluringly set out on rails. Did I think about buying my mother a present? I'm afraid not! We went to the make-up counter and the lady gave us beauty tips and advice and free squirts of perfume. I learned the important skill of applying lipstick.

'You need to have a steady hand,' she said, 'and go right into the corners of your mouth.'

'We're going to a *ceilidhe* tomorrow night in Moran's Hotel,' said Kathleen suddenly. 'Would you like that?'

Would I like it? It would be heaven! Would my mother approve? This was no time for scruples. There was work to be done.

Kathleen helped me to make myself up like the lady in the shop showed me. I didn't do a great job with the mascara and eye shadow. Still I hardly recognised myself in the mirror with the pale, powdered face and red lips. I put on the white dress again and we headed for the dance. It was great night! I learned how to do a Siege of Ennis and the Haymaker's Jig and the two-hand reel. Kathleen had been there before and introduced me to some of her friends. The fellows in the band were lively and full of life, the sweat rolling down their faces as they belted out reels and jigs. We danced all night and one man told me I was a natural. What a shame I wouldn't be there the following Sunday night, he said. After all the exertion and excitement, I was on cloud nine.

I went to see the school in Crumlin where Kathleen was teaching. She had a huge class of sixty inner city children who scrutinized me from top to bottom. I don't know how she kept them under control! She was also involved in a club run by the Legion of Mary called *An Réalt,* where I was warmly welcomed by all the *Gaeilgóirí.* I sang a song and danced and chatted '*as gaeilge*'

All in all, it was a hectic few days and now, at least I would have

Kathleen and Ann in the 1960s

some news to report when I got back to boarding school. When I got home, my father was cutting wood in the yard. He looked disapprovingly at me.

'Is that what they taught you in Dublin? To be putting that red stuff on your mouth. You better wash it off quick before anyone sees you.'

I was back to being a good girl again.

A MOMENT OF MADNESS

There is only a certain time in your life when you can afford to be reckless and mad and not consider the consequences of your actions, when you throw caution to the wind and just live in the moment . . .

It was a warm evening at the end of June and my sister Kathleen and I had big plans. Tonight was the night for the open-air dance stage, four miles away. Hair was discreetly washed and our best dresses laid out in readiness.

Now, the nuns where I went to school, had strenuously denounced this same stage, as a serious occasion of sin, to be avoided at peril to our souls. My mother wasn't quite as strict. Wouldn't it be all local lads that would be there? Fellows you might see going in to Mass on a Sunday. And it would be over early as well. We'd almost be home with the light. My parents were going somewhere that same night, so we couldn't have the use of the car.

The family rosary had to be said before we took off on the bicycle for the dance. Wobbling dangerously from side to side, me steering, Kathleen on the carrier, we arrived breathless with exertion and excitement. The strains of the music from the accordion player could be heard for miles – 'Oh the wayward wind, is a restless wind' and 'A white sports coat and a pink carnation'.

We waited in delicious anticipation for offers. We picked our way through the intricate steps of the Siege of Ennis. We waltzed and tangoed with shy local boys and the occasional more forward stranger, sometimes almost falling off the edge of the stage as the crowd pushed and jostled. We changed partners regularly, refusing all offers of walks, minerals and the 'going home.' Just as we were considering it was time to leave, our next-door neighbour, Margaret, appeared.

'I'm going to the Mayflower ballroom in Mitchelstown. Would you like to come?'

In a moment of madness, without thinking about anything but the prospect of prolonging the night, we agreed.

'What about the bicycle?' asked Kathleen.

'Oh, I'll just tie it on the back of the car and we'll drop it inside your gate. Sure, won't we be passing it on the way?' laughed our resourceful neighbour.

So off we went, to the first proper ballroom I'd even been to. There was a huge crowd and not a single face I recognised. The band were a bunch of attractive young men dressed in white suits, who jumped energetically around the stage, while expertly playing trombones, saxophones and guitars at the same time! The singer was swinging his hips provocatively as he gripped the microphone, blasting out all the popular songs of romance and desire. What would the nuns say if they could see me now?

Smiling couples, heads together, were drinking minerals in the balcony. Others were locked in a slow waltz. The girls standing by the wall were giggling or smoking, pretending to ignore the fellows and the fact that they weren't dancing. Some rushed for the ladies' room to repair make-up and plan new strategies. There was a big revolving ball of light in the ceiling, throwing strange shadows. This was surely the stuff of dreams. Kathleen was already on the floor, her fashionably full-skirted dress billowing out around her as she danced a quickstep. The air was throbbing to the rhythm of the music. The excitement and expectation of the teeming mob was palpable.

When an oily-haired youth with a white sports coat asked me to dance, I threw caution to the wind. He told me I was the most beautiful girl in the ballroom. Well, at least he had good taste, I decided! We danced slow dances, when I nearly broke my arm trying to keep him at a safe distance and fast jive numbers, where I nearly broke my ankles as he twisted and twirled me around in all directions! In between he showered me with compliments, expressing an opinion that I could easily end up in Hollywood.

It all ended on a sour note, however, when I declined the walk and the visit to the mineral bar. You see, the nuns had me well-indoctrinated after all. Anyway, my father had always warned me about fellows with oily hair and white sports coats, and it was all too much bother. I'd stick with the nuns' advice for the moment and leave the occasions of sin for another time . . .

When we got home in the small hours, all hell broke loose. I knew when I saw the light on in the kitchen, the fire lighting, and both my parents still up that we were in trouble. My mother was furious.

'What were you thinking of, staying out till this hour. We were expecting you home hours ago and were worried to death. You could be lying dead in a ditch for all we knew. And you, Kathleen, just because you're working in Dublin doesn't mean that you can lead this *óinseach* astray as well as yourself.' She pointed at me.

My mother ranted and raved, reminding me of what a good-for-nothing I was. I decided that now wouldn't be a good time to discuss my acting career in Hollywood with her! I felt a pang of guilt for being so selfish and causing such worry. Still, I couldn't regret my introduction to the grown-up world of romance and intrigue that I discovered that night in my ballroom of romance!

LIFE IN FLATLAND

Dublin in the swinging sixties! Bee-hive hairdos and double decker buses; the Twist and the Hucklebuck with Brendan Bowyer in the Olympic ballroom; mini-skirts, swing coats and queuing for the cinema.

In my young days, it was called a flat. Now it's an apartment. Which ever name you gave it, it spelt freedom and debauchery, asking men in for tea and being away from home. It also meant that, sometimes, the cupboard was bare and there was no Mammy there to feed you! My father maintained that frying pans and flats went together. They both signalled fast food and loose living!

After years of irritating intrusion from nosy neighbours at home, who knew everyone's business, I basked in sublime urban anonymity. The occupants of the flat below me didn't mind if I was gone to Mass or to the dogs. I could be hungry, or depressed, or dead in my bed, and they couldn't care less! My first experience of flatland in the sixties was, however, very cushioned, as I was sharing with my older sister, Kathleen, who was as good as a mother to me. Apart from doing the cooking, she looked after me in many other ways. She once knit me a lovely fairisle jumper, and I remember hopping impatiently from one foot to the other for her to put the finishing touches to it, so I could wear it to a dance. I mustn't have been pulling my weight, though. In exasperation, she eventually complained to our mother that she had to pay me to clean the cooker!

We had two lovely rooms with bathroom and a resident landlady, who never interfered with our privacy. But then, we were exemplary tenants! Except for one never-to-be-forgotten incident! I had met a young man at a dance, who was training to be a teacher in England. We started corresponding and he arranged to visit, along with his friend.

We were all excited and made the good old reliable Rice Krispie buns. I even cleaned the flat without being paid! We waited all night for the two boys and when they eventually arrived, they were hung over and tired after the boat crossing. All was going well until our lovely landlady, who had such a high opinion of us, knocked on our door and said quietly, 'Could you tell your friend to get out of my bed?'

That was the end of a beautiful romance, I can tell you. Lucky for us that the landlady didn't throw us out as well! It was here that I celebrated my 21st birthday with a party for about 10 people The food consisted of two chickens, sent in the post by my mother, and the music was a record of Billy Vaughan. There was no alcohol. Our youthful exuberance provided enough lift and excitement. Except that I couldn't be too exuberant, as I'd sprained my ankle that evening, getting off the bus! After spending the previous week plucking up the courage to ask this hunk from work to come, I had to watch my friend dancing all night with him. Here, once more, my sister saved the night and made the occasion memorable as I wallowed in self-pity She prepared the chicken sandwiches, baked a cake and made Rice Krispie buns. She had made our sitting-room festive and welcoming and attended to our guests. We all had a great night of innocent fun!

Small wonder then, that I was more than a little aggrieved, when said sister upped and married her Dublin boyfriend and left me high and dry! My cosy life was suddenly turned on its head and I was forced to fend for myself. In reply to an advertisement, I found a 'bedsitter' in South Circular Road. My mother had bigger cupboards at home. The 'kitchen' was a little shelf with a breakfast cooker, beside the wardrobe. The single bed took up most of the rest of the room. To add to my problems, I discovered I had a resident mouse, which was quite terrifying, considering how small the space was. You might find it surprising for a farm girl to have a fear like this, but I remember my mother hated mice as well.

In a fit of pique, at being so cruelly abandoned, and mouse infested, I started knitting a jumper. The momentum of my anger about coincided with the wool running out, at which stage I lost interest in the project.

My sister rescued the knitting and finished it herself! But I still had the problem of the scary rodent! Having scouted around the dance halls of Dublin looking for a mouse catcher, never mind a husband, I finally had to settle for a stray cat I found on the street outside the house. The cat was reluctant, to say the least, so I was forced to lock him in with the pots and pans. He caught no mouse but kept me awake all night, trying to claw his way out. Eventually, I think the mouse found richer pickings in the aromatic flat next door, owned by an Indian gentleman.

Did I mention that I was the only white person in the house? The landlady obviously made more money from renting to black people. Remember this was the sixties. When my mother came to visit and saw Africans and Asians rambling upstairs and down hallways, she was more than a little put out. Especially as Shan Mohangi, who owned a restaurant nearby, called 'The Green Tureen' had just been arrested, for murdering his girlfriend, Hazel Mullen, only the previous month! My mother ordered me to find another flat as soon as possible, as she feared for my safety and her own peace of mind. I remember being so impoverished that I didn't own either a clock or a watch and had to go out to the church across the road to find out the time in the morning!

I found a safe haven in a house in Harold's Cross, with a resident landlady who carefully monitored my comings and goings. She noted if friends, especially the male variety, stayed late and knocked politely on my door to tell me to send them home. My mother must have been saying a novena! On a positive note, I made a life-long friend of the landlady's daughter, Carmel, and we went to many dances together.

Later on, I shared a flat with Mary, an old school friend of mine. She had been working in the bank in Middleton and was transferred to Dublin. We had neither money nor sense, but compensated with optimism and high spirits. We enjoyed ourselves magnificently. Food wasn't important, so money was kept for dances instead. I occasionally bought an egg in the local shop on my way home from work, just to keep the life in me.

I never had great ambitions to climb the corporate ladder. Not that I was overwhelmed with offers mind! My government job paid for my lifestyle and was a place to go each day to socialise with friends and make arrangements for the next night out. Most of the staff were country people, like myself, so I felt right at home. I would sing while I worked and a friend at the other side of the office harmonised. An older member of staff complained that she couldn't concentrate, but the boss just asked me to 'tone it down a bit'!

An old lady, who lived near us at home, once asked me if I had a maid in Dublin to get my meals and lay out my clothes. She was surely living in the dark ages. Any maid I'd engage would have died of the hunger! It was always handy if one of us had a boyfriend, with a car, when we were changing flats, to take our bits and pieces to the new place. One time, we were moving so often, that a particular fellow considered that it would be easier to leave everything in his car until we had finally made up our minds. Eventually we found a lovely, self-contained flat, consisting of a twin-bedded room, kitchen, sitting room and bathroom. This was luxury, not having to share with others in the house. And having no landlady was the icing on the cake. Think of the great parties we could have. And we did. It was hard work, especially cleaning up afterwards, while nursing sore heads and wondering why we bothered.

Then there were the girly nights at home, when we rested between dances and discussed our latest conquests, or lack of them. Men were always up for discussion. We would swear we were sick to death of every last one of them and that we'd enter the convent or emigrate. Next night, we'd be off dancing again!

When my mother came to stay, I had everything in order and a big clean-up done. Once, I took her to a film in the city, but she disapproved of all the love scenes. Next time, I said I'd be more careful, so I brought her to the cartoon cinema in Grafton Street. She told my sister that I had very strange taste in films.

My sister, Eileen, sometimes visited for the week-end. Though she got a warm welcome and was taken to various dances, she didn't get much to eat and complained to my mother. The next time she came, I told her not to be hungry any more, because everything she wanted was in the shop down the road. Food wasn't top of my priority list obviously!

Fellows were always interested in girls who lived in flats with no landladies. There might be a cup of tea or coffee going! One night we had neither and I gave our escort two spoons of a stale cough bottle. I think the reason he opened his mouth so willingly was that he believed he was getting some kind of aphrodisiac! There was a choice of Showbands to dance to and you could be out every night, if you had the energy and the money. There was Laurel Park, the Television Club, Clery's, the Metropole, the Irish Club, the Crystal, the Ierne and the National. This ballroom was for the 'culchies' who were up for the matches and we considered that we were long past that stage! Rock-and-Roll and the Twist were the rage at the time, as well as the more conventional ballroom dances, and it was all very exciting and exhausting.

Sometimes the girls outnumbered the men so we had to take fairly drastic steps to get noticed. This involved getting rid of the eyebrows that we were born with and re-locating them to a loftier and more seductive position. Our eyes were ringed with black pencil and this, together with our white powdered faces, gave us a koala bear look. We honestly believed that this would be the pattern of our lives forever. That we'd always be twenty-five! We could carry on being gloriously self-absorbed and irresponsible. On the occasional visits back to the old thatched house, I would, very often, have to get my bus fare back to Dublin from my mother. Of course, I thought that she was lucky to be honoured with my presence at all!

I doubt that I could afford a flat in Dublin these days. Would I want to be twenty-five again? With the ballrooms and show-bands consigned to history, maybe not. But we did have our moment in the sun!

A NIGHT TO REMEMBER

The beauty of the great outdoors and the heather clad peaks was very quickly lost on Beloved when cold and hunger set in. All he wanted was to get down off the mountain, have a hot shower and a greasy fry-up!

I had been planning it for weeks and now the right moment had come. The weather forecast was favourable and the equipment had been checked out. The sleeping bags and tent had shoulder straps for ease of carriage. A flashlight, cassette radio, two books, biscuits and water completed the packing. Now, to break the news to Beloved! It was a beautiful sunny June afternoon and he was tidying up in the garden. These matters are always better presented as a fait accompli.

'How about us climbing the Galtees together this evening and spending the night? It should be perfect. The forecast is good.'

'Are you serious? Yes, I can see that you are. What if there's fog, or we die with the cold'.

'Don't be such a baby. It's June, for God's sake. This will be a really wonderful experience. A chance to find ourselves. Out there with God, and nature, and the silence of the mountain!'

'Find ourselves, is it? More likely, we'll end up lost.'

We set off, driving up the 'black road' to the point where the mountain ascent begins. We were in high spirits, the gear neatly strapped to our backs, the beauty of nature spread out around us. I was glad we'd worn light clothes as now, with the climb getting tougher, we were beginning to get hot and sweaty. We stopped here and there to admire the purple, heathery peaks and listen to the musical tinkle of the little mountain streams. Far down below, I spotted the outline of the old farmhouse, the sun reflecting on its golden thatch.

Beloved was in great glee, remarking that we should do this more often and that he was glad I had suggested it. He could see what I meant about the beauty of the great outdoors. The odd sheep glanced curiously at us, but otherwise we had the Galtees to ourselves. The sun was still high in the sky and we had about two hours climbing ahead of us. Beloved was still in fine form and we felt a mutual spiritual bond, confronting this great challenge together. Having lived in the shadow of this great mountain for so long, I couldn't wait to spend one unforgettable night on her summit.

Overseen by a flock of sheep, we pitched our tent on a reasonably flat plateau. I was glad of the all-in-one ground sheet, which protected us from creepie-crawlies and sheep droppings.

As we sorted out our sleeping quarters I noticed, with dismay, that our sleeping bags were paper thin, the type suited to a continental climate. Come to think of it, that's where our daughters had used them last. Now, light is great for transportation, but not good for insulation on top of Galtymore!

'Why didn't you bring a warm quilt anyway?' asked Beloved, crossly, gazing with horror at his flimsy covering.

'Why do you think?' I snapped. 'Maybe I should have brought mattresses, pillows and blankets as well. This is a camping expedition, you can't expect the comforts of home'

It was only eight o'clock, but there was nothing for it but to zip up and settle down for the night. Putting on the radio, we lay back to enjoy the music and the solitude. As it got dark, we read by the light of the flash-lamp. This is the life, I thought – something to tell our grandchildren. Suddenly the torch flickered and then the radio faded.

'Why the hell didn't you bring batteries?'

'Why didn't you bring them? I can't be expected to remember everything, can I?'

Curious sheep, attracted by the loud voices, were pushing against the tent, which was perilously close to falling apart. Beloved was shivering audibly and feeling very sorry for himself. I was freezing, but not about to admit it!

'Have you anything to eat?'

The biscuits and water failed to appease him.

'This is worse than Lough Derg,' he moaned.

'Well offer it up for your sins then, and you'll get some good out of it. Anyway,' I added consolingly, 'just wait 'til the morning and you see the magnificent view. It will be all worthwhile.'

'Bull . . .' spat Beloved, who was getting less beloved by the second. 'I'll get my death up here on this bloody mountain over you. I should never have listened to you.'

It really was cold. With two separate bags, snuggling up to generate heat was not an option. Anyway, snuggling was the last thing on my mind at that moment. Now, divorce . . .

'Will it be bright soon,' he muttered through chattering teeth. I had dozed in a fitful, nightmarish kind of way and woke with a start.

Then I heard the patter of rain. 'Isn't that nice?' I remarked enthusiastically. 'The sound of the rain on the tent!'

'What's bloody nice about it?' snorted Grumpy. 'It just means that now, on top of all our misery, we'll be soaked going home. The next time you get any bright ideas for adventure trips – GO ON YOUR OWN!'

'You bet I will – the sheep are better company than you.'

At last the light came. I failed to deliver on the beautiful view. The grey fog and overcast sky were less than inspiring. The tent was silently dismantled and we started down the mountain, me trailing by a half a mile! The sleeping bags were thrown over our shoulders to protect us from the deluge. When we arrived home around 5 a.m., our spirits lifted somewhat as the house wrapped us in its familiar comfort. It's amazing what a big fry-up can do for a man. The blanched, tortured look gradually disappeared as power was restored to all systems! When you think about it, aren't men's needs simple enough, really!

After the second cup of tea, he even got back his 'Beloved' title again.

MY JOURNEY BACK...

Towards the end of the swinging sixties I decided to leave my good, pensionable job as a clerk in the Eastern Health Board and move to the USA. It was a new experience, meeting and mixing with American girls. I worked in a similar position, as an office clerk with a health insurance firm, and everybody was very helpful.

I visited my father's oldest sister, who was a nun in Vermont. None of our family had ever met her, since she left Ireland in the twenties. I stayed the night in a convent cell and had four Tipperary nuns watching me eat my breakfast the next morning and enjoying my brogue! I also went to see Aunt Esther, who was now in her eighties. But she still had a twinkle in her eye! She lived near enough to Aunt Ciss in Dorchester, Boston, so I did the rounds of relations and cousins!

Within a couple of years, I was married with a new baby daughter, Kelley, and comfortably settled in New Haven, Connecticut. I thought my course in life was set. My husband, Bobby Gardiner, is an Irish traditional accordion player from near Lisdoonvarna in Co. Clare. We had met a couple of years previously at an Irish music function. Our wedding reception was in a well-known hotel in Dublin and, even though it was St. Patrick's Day, the staff didn't want Irish music played in the bar, in case it would disturb the other guests! Thankfully, a lot has changed. I was enlisted as the fourth member of his Country and Irish music group and we did gigs every week-end, sometimes travelling to Boston and New York. Here I was, with a lovely first baby, a grand new husband and a chance to sing. Could life get any better?

I loved the Americans. They were warm, welcoming, funny, honest, generous and encouraging. I think we could learn a lot from them. I got loads of baby gifts from people I hardly knew. I ate pizza for the first time. Foods like corn, peppers, hot dogs, potato salad and pretzels were tried out. I got to like visiting 'Dunkin' Donuts'! I learned strange words relating to baby paraphernalia, like diapers, pacifiers, strollers, cribs, formula, receiving blankets! Americans pronounce all babies to be 'adorable'. (For a while I thought that Kelley was the only one!) I basked in the delight and convenience of washers, dryers and colour televisions. When I was doing the late baby feed, I thought how marvellous it was to have all night chat shows and soaps to keep me company. At home, RTE didn't come on until evening!

I sometimes took music engagements. On one occasion, a lady called up and asked if she could have Bobby Gardiner's Irish orchestra to play for her daughter's wedding! Apparently anything more than three pieces was considered to be an orchestra. Sure, aren't the Yanks famous for exaggerating! I was quite nervous about singing on stage at first but soon got used to it. The Americans were happy once you sang 'Danny Boy'. Their weddings were very elaborate affairs with garter rituals, bouquet throwing and a lot of pomp and ceremony. It's much the same in Ireland nowadays. I was heartily sick of weddings after the first couple of dozen.

We sometimes had bar-b-q's in friends' yards on the lovely, hot summer days and this, too, was a novelty (including the hot summer days!). In my childhood, my mother might have given us a cup of tea in the orchard as a treat. But this was a whole meal, with hamburgers, hot dogs and chicken cooked over charcoal. The mosquitoes were the only problem. They loved my rich Irish blood. Life was going merrily by and I was enjoying every minute of it. I was almost able to 'talk American'. Then, out of the blue, a letter arrived from my mother.

She had been widowed a few years at this stage and found the running of the place too much. Would we come home and take over the farm? I had never seen myself as a farmer and, though my husband was from farming stock too, he had abandoned all that years before. After much soul searching, we decided to return. After the glamour and excitement of life in the US coming back to the quiet, rural Ireland of the early seventies, which was still in the dark ages in

many respects, was a great culture shock. Bobby was appalled at the
telephone service, where you had to twirl a handle and hope the lady
in the post office would answer you! I found the apathy and reserve
of the people a little disappointing, after the passion and enthusiasm
I had left behind. Nobody was interested in hearing about what you'd
seen or where you'd been. If you greeted them with a kiss, they were
slightly alarmed. I quickly learned it was best to keep my head down
and get rid of any American habits I'd adopted!

I went back to washing clothes by hand and trying to dry them between
the showers! Running water and indoor toilets were only starting to
come into the country places. I felt I had taken a major step backwards.
For Bobby's first music engagement after returning from America, he
received the princely sum of two pounds in Fermoy, Co. Cork. He felt
like taking the next plane back! But, at least, it got us going on the
music circuit again. We did the rounds of the ballad lounges, which were
at their height, and travelled long distances to many parts of Munster.
We started the afternoon sessions in 'The Silver Sand' a lounge outside
Cahir. The fee for two hours was four pounds! We played regularly in
places like Kilmaley and Kilmihill, where Bobby blasted out reel after
reel to satisfy the energetic, frenzied Clare set dancers. I was very lucky
to have two great baby-sitters, as well as my mother. Sometimes we
wouldn't get back until three or four in the morning.

I think my mother was never fully reconciled to us having a music
group and playing in lounges and pubs. It somehow didn't seem a
respectable way to make a living! However, she came along with us a
few times to see what it was all about. Two more children, Fiodhna
and Lynda, arrived later in the seventies to complete our family. I
took the three of them to piano lessons and Irish dancing classes. It
was a good way to meet the neighbours. Although I was from the
area, many of the people I'd known as a child were now either dead
or had moved away, so you could say that I was getting re-acquainted
with my own place again.

We had built a bungalow a field away from the old thatched house
after returning from the U.S.A. so we were within calling distance of

my mother. She kept herself busy in the garden and also turned out some beautiful knitting and crotchet. Reading was her great love, too, until her sight began to fail. She was a committed Catholic, faithful to Mass and the rosary to the end.

The open fire had to be tended constantly and became almost like a friend to her. Bobby ensured that she was supplied with lots of wood from the trees on the farm. However, she was always afraid that a big blaze would set the house alight! I took her to town every week, where she insisted on doing her own shopping. Her travel pass was frequently used when she went on visits to family members, especially to Dublin to visit Kathleen. But she was happiest at home. She lived out her days, almost to the end, in the old thatched house, which, apart from a few improvements, was much the same as when I was a child. It was newly thatched in 1973 by a local craftsman who was 80-years-old at the time. It was re-thatched in the nineties by a German lady!

The children were growing up and learning to play music, too. As they improved, they were drafted into the group. They loved the novelty at first, but as they got older they had their own interests and music preferences and it was no longer considered 'cool'. However, they retained a great love for traditional music and each is still proficient on her own instrument. They also learned how to teach music at a young age and served their time as Bobby's apprentices, when he taught on Saturdays in Stradbally, Kilmacthomas and Waterford city. It was a handy way for them to earn an extra bit of pocket money and a good preparation for their future careers.

Our children's visits to my mother kept her going, and she always had packets of crisps and treats hidden away. They gained an important insight, too, into the old Ireland – the open fire with the big chimney through which you could see the sky. And then there was the machine, with the wheel you turned to blow the fire and the old stairs up to the loft where we had slept as children. Because it was just a field away, they could safely ramble up to see her almost as soon as they could walk! Santa Claus came to the old thatched house again. My poor mother would be wakened at all hours on Christmas morning with an excited knock on the door to get in to see what Santa had brought. She often looked after them when we made return visits to America and other places, and was a very kind and caring granny. The wealth of stories that she made up to keep them entertained added a precious, rich dimension to their lives.

In 1990, we got the opportunity to travel to Switzerland as a family group. We shared the stage with The Hot House Flowers, The Black Velvet Band and Brian Kennedy. It was a once-in-a-life-time occasion that we will always remember. Our girls grew up into fine young women and all three went into the teaching profession. Two are living and working in the Middle East and Kelley, our 'Yank', is teaching in Dungarvan, Co. Waterford.

Over the years, John, Kathleen and Eileen kept in touch with home and all the cousins met and got to know each other there. Of course, when my mother died, the heart of the house died with her. We rented the old house for a number of years after her death, but because none of the family wanted to live there, we decided to put it up for sale. Since it's a listed building, the thatched roof will have to be retained and maintained and any other improvements carried out would be subject to planning permission from the County Council. It's a project for a younger person.

I'd say my brother, John, was very relieved to have the burden of becoming a farmer taken from his shoulders! It certainly was not his calling. We tried our hand at rearing cattle in the early years. However, as time went by and Bobby, together with his regular commitments, began travelling overseas with Cómhaltas Ceoilteóiri Éireann, we decided to lease the land.

So now I return you to the dairy, where I started my nostalgia trip. However, nothing stays the same. The new owner decided to make a sound recording studio to indulge his music hobby from this old dusty shed. It housed all our family mementos and memories for dozens of years, but now it has a whole new purpose!

I wonder if the spirits of the past still linger there.